(**cap-puc-cino**); Latin languages seem here to be systematically different from Germanic (Delattre, 1971). The phonetic difference is a matter of subtleties of timing, and it is therefore interesting in the context of handedness (McManus & Cornish, 1997) that the perception and production of geminates may be cerebellar in origin (Ivry & Gopal, 1993).

What about **asymmetry**? Is there a particular problem with that word? Here accurate information is relatively easy to find. A few years ago I searched MedLine and PsycLit and produced the following statistics:

	PsycLit	*MedLine*
asymmetry	2935	8311
assymmetry	4	16
asymetry	1	32
assymetry	10	38

The papers cited in MedLine seem to be marginally more likely to make the errors. Surprisingly all three erroneous forms are fairly prevalent, and these are probably lower bounds on their occurrence since editors, proof readers and spell checking software will no doubt have weeded out many others before they arrive in print. Lest it be worried that these problems are errors of re-keying at MedLine and PsycLit, a few examples will show that is not the case. A paper in *Nature* (Lowe et al., 1996) managed to have ***asymetric*** in its table 1, despite having **asymmetric** in the title; John Ziman's book *Reliable Knowledge* (1978) suggested "our universe is uniquely ***assymmetrical***" (p.58); and most bizarrely of all, and probably reflecting a somewhat different type of error, *The Lancet* managed to come up with ***asymmmetry*** (Newton & Seagroatt, 1993)—a so-called perseverative dysgraphia, reported as specific to geminates (Venneri et al., 1994). Errors are not confined to the word **asymmetry** itself. Of interest to workers in laterality, is Schiller's usage, in his biography of Broca, of ***corrolary*** rather than **corollary** (Schiller, 1979); here, as so often seems to be the case, there seems to be some internal cognitive code that the word is somehow asymmetric, meaning that when one letter is doubled, another is shortened in compensation, thereby restoring the asymmetry. In an unusual example where the erroneous form seems to be the norm, in their chapter for the *Blackwell Dictionary of Neuropsychology*, Sandra Witelson and Phil Bryden commented that **dichhaptic** is more often spelled wrongly than rightly (Witelson & Bryden, 1995), as ***dichaptic***—presumably reflecting an incorrect folk etymology, as also occurs for that most frequently mis-spelled of medical words, **pruritus** (McManus, 1995). Finally, lest I might be thought holier than thou, and since I know that Michael Corballis will tell the story if I do not, I remember writing to him in the early 1970s when I was an undergraduate, enclosing a manuscript I had written; the charming letter in reply had the gentlest of admonishments: "you should notice **asymmetry** itself has an asymmetry which you have neglected".

REFERENCES

Delattre, P. (1971). Consonant gemination in four languages: An acoustic, perceptual, and radiographic study: I. *International Review of Applied Linguistics in Language Teaching, 9*, 31–52.

Ivry, R.B., & Gopal, H.-S. (1993). Speech production and perception in patients with cerebellar lesions. In D.E. Meyer & S. Kornblum (Eds.), *Attention and Performance XIV: Synergies in experimental psychology, artificial intelligence, and cognitive neuroscience*. Cambridge, MA: MIT Press.

Lowe, L.A., Supp, D.M., Sampath, K., Yokoyama, T., Wright, C.V.E., Potter, S.S., Overbeek, P., & Kuehn, M.R. (1996). Conserved left-right asymmetry of nodal expression and alterations in murine situs inversus. *Nature, 381*, 158–161.

McManus, I.C. (1980). Handedness in twins: A critical review. *Neuropsychologia, 18*, 347–355.

McManus, I.C. (1995). Pruritus. *Lancet, 345*, 1584.

McManus, I.C., & Cornish, K.M. (1997). Fractionating handedness in mental retardation: What is the role of the cerebellum? *Laterality 2*, 81–90.

Newton, J., & Seagroatt, V. (1993). Why is osteoarthritis of the hip more common on the right? *Lancet, 341*, 179.

Schiller, F. (1979). *Paul Broca: Explorer of the brain*. Oxford: Oxford University Press.

Venneri, A., Cubelli, R., & Caffarra, P. (1994). Perseverative dysgraphia: A selective disorder in writing double letters. *Neuropsychologia, 32*, 923–931.

Witelson, S.F., & Bryden, M.P. (1995). Dichhaptic technique. In G. Beaumont, P. Kenealy, & M. Rogers (Eds.) *The Blackwell dictionary of neuropsychology* (pp. 270–274). Oxford: Blackwell.

Ziman, J. (1978). *Reliable knowledge: An exploration of the grounds for belief in science*. Cambridge: Cambridge University Press.

LATERALITY, 1999, *4* (3), 193–196

Of Geminates and Gemellology

Chris McManus

University College London, UK

Twins have always attracted attention—Romulus and Remus, Castor and Pollux, Jacob and Esau, Fafner and Fasold; there has always been intrigue, mystery and confusion surrounding two-in-one and one-in-two. The interest for *Laterality* and lateralisation is compounded, because if it is the difference between an individual's two sides that results in laterality, how are those two sides represented in twins, particularly monozygotic twins that once were one? This Special Issue of *Laterality* clearly indicates a continuing interest in the relationship of twinning and laterality, and it is a particular pleasure to include both biological and neuropsychological papers. The editors' job has been particularly easy since all but one of the papers were submitted spontaneously, and the only editorial tasks were the pleasant ones of putting them together, and writing a light-hearted introduction to accompany the heavier but extremely interesting scientific fare that follows. Finally, although I've long been interested in twins professionally (McManus, 1980), I now have two more reasons for fascination. The ultrasound scan below, at fourteen weeks of gestation, shows the first glimpse of our daughters Franziska and Anna, born on June 25th 1999 just as the journal went to press. This Special Issue is dedicated to them and to Christine.

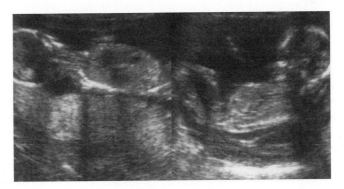

Requests for reprints should be sent to Professor I.C. McManus, Dept of Psychology, University College London, Gower Street, London WC1E 6BT, UK.

I am grateful to Professor Brian Butterworth and Dr Marco Zorzi, for their help while preparing this editorial.

The problems of asymmetry and twinning start even with the very words themselves. Both words are what are called 'geminates', the term derived from the Latin verb *geminare* (to double), and hence *geminus*, meaning twin (as in the Gemini of the zodiac), and *gemellus*, the diminutive form. A geminate is therefore a word with twinned letters (although there are also technical meanings in botany, architecture, chemistry and molecular genetics). Geminate words sometimes but not always produce spelling problems[1] for the unwary, particularly when, as in **asymmetry**, the English pronunciation would hardly be changed if all the letters were double or single: ***asymetry**, ***assymetry**, **asymmetry** and ***assymmetry** would all be spoken in an essentially similar way. The correct spelling is therefore particularly difficult to remember (unlike a word such as **twinning**, which if it were spelled as **twining** would be pronounced with a long rather than a short 'i'). As a result geminates have always been particular favourites for school spelling tests, and those of us drilled to spell words such as **accommodation**, still wince on seeing ***accommodation** and ***accomodation** on almost every student notice board. Particularly distressing is that there is undoubtedly an exposure effect, repeated occurrences of the wrong spelling eventually making one doubts one's own memory and go scurrying back to the dictionary for reassurance.

Problems with geminates are surprisingly pervasive. The London *Independent on Sunday* (1996, 12th May, p. 16) told two related geminate stories. The more benign merely embarrassed the Reuters News Agency who in a memorably erroneous and pointless correction announced: "In Colombo story headlined 'Sri Lanka **desiccated** coconut sector future unclear' please read in headline and second para ... **desiccated** coconut ... instead of ***dessicated** coconut"[2]. The second story concerned a drugs smuggler who had the bright idea of importing hashish in tin cans, each of which had its own carefully printed labels identifying it as "***dessicated** coconut". Unfortunately the Customs Officer could spell properly, and immediately got out his can opener...

Foreign geminates can be particularly problematic: London cafes and restaurants currently have an epidemic of selling ***capuccino**, rather than **cappuccino**; my local restaurant even has ***rissoto** rather than **risotto**. The problem is that the double letters are phonemic in Italian—they are pronounced differently from single letters, and that matters in a language with strict grapheme-phoneme translations. Italians therefore find it easier to know how to spell them (or at least I have yet to see a ***capuccino** for sale in Italy). From a linguistic point of view these phonemic geminates are treated as two separate consonants, one attached to the previous vowel, and one to the following vowel

---

[1] To avoid confusion, I will adopt the traditional linguistic nomenclature of putting an asterisk in front of words which are not legitimate spellings, and when words are being discussed as words will put them in bold.

[2] I have added emboldening and asterisks in all quotations.

LATERALITY, 1999, *4* (3), 197–208

Twinning and Embryonic Left–Right Asymmetry

Michael Levin

Harvard Medical School, USA

COMMENTARY

The geometrical invariance known as symmetry is a striking feature of developmental morphology during embryogenesis. The left–right axis of an animal's body plan is often thought of as being fundamentally different from the dorso-ventral and antero-posterior axes because of the symmetry that it exhibits when viewed from the outside. Interestingly though, the internal organs of most animals reveal an individually and evolutionarily conserved asymmetry which requires patterning of the same order of complexity as the other two axes. Animal body-plans occur in a wide variety of symmetries such as spherical, radial, and bilateral. Vertebrates have a generally bilaterally symmetrical body-plan, but this symmetry is broken further into a pseudo-symmetry by the consistently asymmetric placement of various internal organs such as the heart, liver, spleen, and gut, or an asymmetric development of paired organs (such as brain hemispheres or lungs). I limit this discussion to include only *invariant* (i.e. consistent among all normal individuals of a given type) differences between the left and right sides of an animal's morphology. This specifically excludes pseudo-random characteristics such as animal coat colours, and minor stochastic deviations due to developmental noise.

The LR axis itself follows automatically from the definition of the AP and DV axes, as it is perpendicular to both; however, consistently imposed asymmetry across it is fundamentally different from patterning along the other two axes. First, whereas the AP and DV axes can be set by exogenous cues such as gravity, or sperm entry point, there is no independent way to pick out the left (or right) direction, as no obvious macroscopic aspect of nature differentiates left from right. Second, all normal members of a given species are asymmetrical in the *same* direction. However, animals with complete mirror reversal of internal organs can arise (*situs inversus*) and are otherwise phenotypically unimpaired. Thus, although it is possible to come up with plausible evolutionary reasons why organisms might be asymmetric in the first place (optimal packing

---

Requests for reprints should be sent to Michael Levin, Bldg. C1, 5th floor, Cell Biology Dept., Harvard Medical School, 240 Longwood Avenue, Boston, MA 02115, USA.
Email: levin@whiz.med.harvard.edu

---

of viscera, etc.), there is no obvious reason why they should all be asymmetric in the same direction. It is, after all, much easier to imagine a developmental mechanism for generating asymmetry (such as positive-feedback and amplification of stochastic biochemical differences) than for biasing it to a given direction. The left–right axis thus presents several unique and deeply interesting theoretical issues.

Several model systems have contributed to the study of LR asymmetry (see Fujinaga, 1996; Levin, 1997; Levin & Mercola, 1998a; Wood, 1997) for general reviews on LR asymmetry). It has long been known (Burn, 1991; Winer-Muram, 1995) that human beings occasionally present loss of LR asymmetry (isomerism), complete reversals of the normal asymmetry (*situs inversus*), or partial reversals of symmetry (heterotaxia). Several strains of vertebrates and invertebrates that recapitulate these syndromes (Hummel & Chapman, 1959; Mochizuki et al., 1998; Supp, Witte, Potter, & Brueckner, 1997; Yokoyama et al., 1993) as well as a list of pharmacological agents that cause *situs* defects in mammalian embryos are known (Levin, 1997). *Drosophila*, which has provided molecular entry points into so many other biological phenomena through classical genetics, has not been a factor in LR research because it has a very low degree of asymmetry (manifest only as the chiral nature of the rotation of the male sex organ and the testicular outflow tract [Polani, 1996, but see Martin-Blanco & Garcia-Bellido, 1996]), and selections for external LR asymmetry have not been successful (Tuinstra, DeJong, & Scharloo, 1990).

Several experiments have shed light on the timing of LR asymmetry specification. Chick heart sidedness has been experimentally demonstrated to be determined during gastrulation (Hoyle, Brown, & Wolpert, 1992); studies on LR inversions induced by drugs likewise suggest that in mammals, a critical period in LR biasing occurs before late gastrulation (Fujinaga & Baden, 1991). Thus it is clear that decisions fundamental to LR asymmetry are made long before any overt signs of morphological asymmetry, and long before the morphogenesis of asymmetric organs.

THE MOLECULAR LEFT–RIGHT PATHWAY

A number of asymmetrically expressed genes have now been described (Levin, 1997). These include a variety of signalling molecules and transcription factors. Figure 1 illustrates the expression pattern of three such genes as assayed by *in situ* hybridisation with riboprobes to the relevant genes: *Sonic Hedgehog* (Shh), *Nodal*, and *PTC* (Levin et al., 1995). *Shh* is expressed only on the left side of Hensen's node in the gastrulating chick embryo. Shortly thereafter, *Nodal* and *PTC* are expressed also on the left side.

Once a set of asymmetrically expressed genes had been identified, their location and relative timing of expression suggested a possible pathway of sequential inductions and repressions. Using artificial retroviruses bearing the

Shh   Nodal   PTC

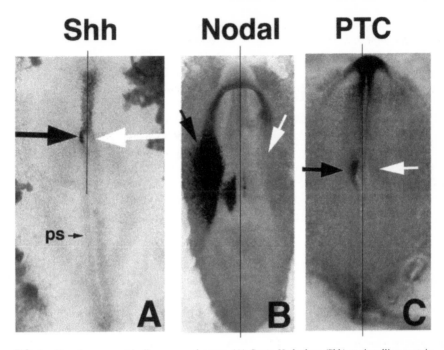

FIG. 1.   Sample asymmetrically expressed genes. (A) *Sonic Hedgehog (Shh)*, a signalling protein involved in patterning the limb and neural tube in vertebrates, is expressed on the left side of Hensen's node as well in the notochord during gastrulation. PS = primitive streak. (B) *Nodal*, a member of the *BMP* superfamily of signalling molecules, is expressed in two domains on the left side of the midline in neurula stage chick embryos. (C) *PTC*, a receptor for the Shh protein is expressed adjacent to Hensen's node on the left side. The thin vertical lines indicate the axis of LR symmetry.

gene of interest or protein-coated beads, a model for the LR pathway was constructed. For example, it was found that misexpressing the normally left-sided gene *Shh* on the right side caused the ectopic right-sided expression of *Nodal*, which is normally also confined to the left side. This cascade (summarised in Fig. 2) begins when *activin* βB becomes expressed on the right side of Hensen's node (st. 3). This soon induces the expression of *Act-RIIa* in the right side, and shuts off the right-side expression of *Shh* (which was previously expressed throughout the node). Soon thereafter, *Shh* (which at that point is expressed only on the left side of the node and in the notochord) induces *PTC* in cells adjacent to the node, and *nodal* in a small domain of cells adjacent to the left side of the node. This is soon followed by a much larger domain of *nodal* expression in the lateral plate mesoderm. *Nodal* then induces the expression of *Pitx2* also on the left side (Logan et al., 1998). *cSNR* is expressed on the right side, and is suppressed by *Nodal* on the left (Isaac, Sargent, & Cooke, 1997).

Most importantly, the early asymmetrically expressed genes are not merely markers of inherent laterality, but play an active role in LR patterning.

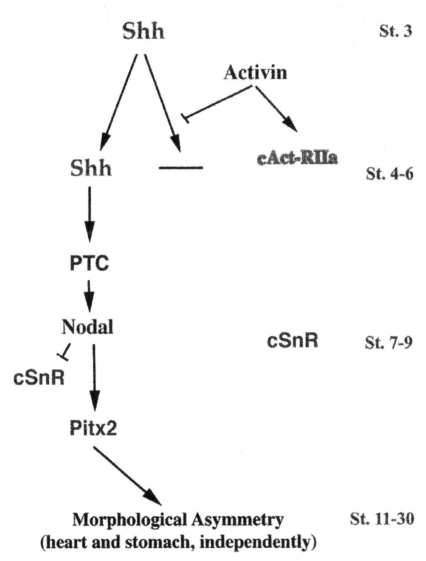

FIG. 2. The pathway of LR-asymmetric genes. *Shh* is initially expressed throughout the node. Right-sided *Activin* expression induces expression of *cAct-RIIa* on the right, and represses *Shh* on the right side of Hensen's node, leaving left-only expression. It then induces left-sided expression of *PTC*, which probably functions to transduce the *Shh* signal to induce *Nodal*, which in turn represses the transcription factor *cSnR* (which stays expressed on the right, where *Nodal* is absent), and induces left-sided *Pitx2*. This leads to proper asymmetric organogenesis in the viscera.

Misexpression of *activin* or *Shh* (which result in missing or bilateral *nodal* expression respectively) specifically randomise heart *situs* in the chick (Levin et al., 1995). Moreover, *nodal*, which is in direct contact with cardiac precursor cells, can reverse heart *situs* or cause symmetric hearts (Levin et al., 1997). The same is true of *Pitx2* (Logan et al., 1998). Thus, although there is no consensus on what causes cardiac looping in the first place, it is plausible that *nodal* or *Pitx2* is instructing heart looping by providing an asymmetric signal to one side of the cardiac primordia, and affecting the proliferation, migration, or cytoskeletal organisation of cardiac precursors. The fact that morphologically normal hearts form in the absence of *Shh* and *nodal* expression (albeit with randomisation of heart *situs*) indicates that the genes in this cascade are neither responsible for inducing heart formation nor for instructing its morphogenesis. Rather, they seem to provide a pivotal influence determining the handedness of the heart. Interestingly, the other organs besides the heart likewise take their cues from this genetic cascade (Levin et al., 1997). Some members of this cascade (such as *Nodal* and *Pitx2*) are clearly involved in LR decisions in the frog and mouse, as well as chick (Collignon, Varlet, & Robinson, 1996; Lowe et al., 1996; Ryan et al., 1998), although the extent of evolutionary conservation of the other parts of the pathway is still unknown (Levin & Mercola, 1998b).

Several other genes that are not asymmetrically expressed but play a role in laterality decisions have been described, but it is currently unknown where in the pathway they fit (Hyatt & Yost, 1998; Levin & Mercola, 1998c; Mochizuki et al., 1998; Supp et al., 1997).

MODELS FOR CONJOINED TWINS AND LATERALITY DEFECTS

Twins and the twinning process have had a relevance for laterality research ever since the tantalising experiments of Spemann (Spemann & Falkenberg, 1919). It has been noted (Burn, 1991; Morrill, 1919; Newman, 1916; Schwind, 1934; Winer-Muram, 1995) that conjoined twins in human beings, mice, and frogs tend to exhibit laterality defects. Whereas the *Xenopus* system makes it very easy to induce twins on demand (Hyatt, Lohr, & Yost, 1996; Nascone & Mercola, 1997), modern workers in the chick system have relied on spontaneous twins.

In reviewing the human literature on conjoined twins, it was observed that only parapagus and thoracopagus twins tend to exhibit *situs* abnormalities (Levin, Roberts, Holmes, & Tabin, 1996); these are twins thought to originate from two adjacent embryonic streaks developing side by side, either in parallel or obliquely (Fig. 3B). Guided by the LR pathway, Levin et al. (1996) examined the expression of the asymmetric genes in analogously positioned chick twins and proposed two models explaining laterality defects found in conjoined twins. These are both based on molecules in the LR pathway crossing some distance in

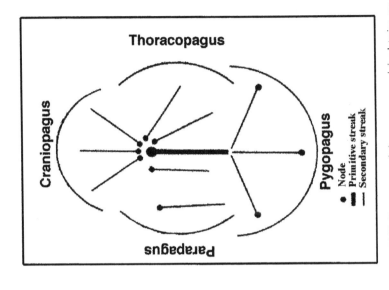

FIG. 3. Human conjoined twins and laterality defects. (A, modified from Arey, 1965) Parapagus and thoracopagus conjoined twins are the only ones associated with laterality defects. (B, modified from Kapur, Jack, & Siebert, 1994; Spencer, 1992, 1995) Side-by-side and oblique arrangements of primitive streaks are thought to give rise to such twins, consistent with models of laterality defects caused by crossover of asymmetric signalling molecules between adjacent primitive streaks.

the blastoderm and affecting the conjoined embryo. The precise details of geometric arrangement and timing determine which members of the LR cascade affect the twin, and thus control which twin exhibits the *situs* anomaly.

For example, in primitive streaks that grow parallel to each other from early stages (Fig. 4A), right-sided sided *activin* in the left streak would inhibit the normal left-sided expression of *Shh* in the right twin. This would lead to absence of *nodal* expression (Fig. 4B) in the right twin, which causes morphological *situs* defects (Levin et al., 1995). When spontaneous chick twins with parallel primitive streaks are examined by *in situ* hybridisation for *Shh* expression, as predicted it is seen that the left twin has normal *Shh* expression but the right twin has a lack of *Shh* expression in the node (Fig. 4C).

In contrast, when primitive streaks arise far apart, but grow towards each other during gastrulation (Fig. 4D), *Shh* expression proceeds normally in both twins. However, during head-fold stages, the *Shh* expression of the right twin induces aberrant *nodal* expression on the right side of the left twin (Fig. 4E). When head-fold stage spontaneous chick twins with oblique streaks are examined for *nodal* expression (Fig. 4F), as predicted it is seen that the right twin has *nodal* expression only on the left side (i.e. normal expression), while the left-most twin has expression (black arrows) on both the left and right sides (which leads to laterality defects, Levin et al., 1995).

The accompanying paper by Dr von Kraft represents a careful and painstaking set of experiments on the relationship between twinning and LR asymmetry. Taking advantage of the fact that conjoined twins can be readily created in *Triturus* by fusing embryos during development, Dr von Kraft examined morphological laterality of twins conjoined in different orientations. Thus, this work represents further, specific experimental tests of the models described earlier. A great advantage of this paradigm for mechanistic studies of LR patterning over systems where twins are created by inducing ectopic axes in an existent embryo (Hyatt et al., 1996; Nascone & Mercola, 1997) is that it avoids additional complexities caused by splitting an embryonic field that already may contain left–right information. Additionally, it allows finer control over the relative ages of the twins.

The studies in *Triturus* present several interesting conclusions. The most fundamental observation is that fusion of embryos results in laterality defects; this clearly demonstrates that splitting of an embryo's left–right field is not required for laterality defects. This is consistent with the chick models which suggest that the asymmetry phenotypes are the result of interference between rather mature streaks, and not a fundamental result of the splitting of the organiser prior to streak formation. Second, the phenotype of the resulting twins is heterotaxia, including all possible permutations of the viscera (many more morphological markers of laterality were scored than in most *Xenopus* or chick studies). Heterotaxia is the phenotype caused by introducing ectopic sources of several of the genes in the LR pathway in chick embryos (Levin et al., 1997).

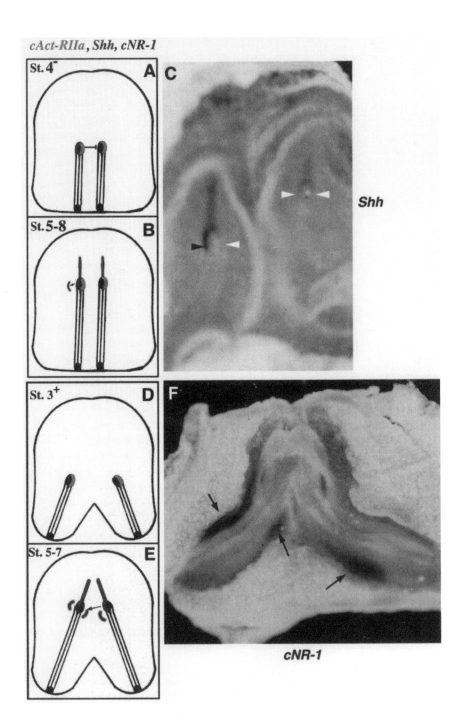

cAct-RIIa, Shh, cNR-1

St. 4⁻   A

St. 5-8   B

C

Shh

St. 3⁺   D

St. 5-7   E

F

cNR-1

204

Third, heterolateral fusion is more effective in causing heterotaxia than homolateral fusion. This result is also predicted by the chick pathway models, which specifically postulate ectopic downstream gene expression caused by influence of left-sided upstream genes on the right side (and vice versa). Fourth, it was found that gastrula and early neurula stages are the most sensitive to laterality defects. These are precisely the stages during which asymmetric genes have been described in the chick. Fifth, which side is seen to be dominant depends on which aspect of laterality one scores. Finally, the effect occurs even when the embryos are of different families of amphibians. This is not surprising given that the asymmetric genes discussed earlier are well conserved signalling molecules present in most animal systems (see Levin & Mercola, 1998b for a discussion of conservation of LR signalling among species).

CHIRALITY ISSUES IN NON-CONJOINED TWINS

The models just discussed present plausible explanations of laterality defects in conjoined twins. There is, however, an interesting set of observations which suggests that they do not tell the whole story, and that even in mammals, chirality is determined as early as the first few cell divisions, and certainly before the streak appears. *Non-conjoined* monozygotic twins, while not exhibiting the kinds of visceral laterality defects that occur in conjoined twins, do manifest many subtler kinds of mirror-image asymmetry ("bookend" or enantiomer twin pairs). Pairs of such twins have been noted to present mirror asymmetries in hand preference, hair whorl direction, tooth patterns, unilateral eye and ear defects, and even tumour locations and un-descended testicles (Beere, Hargreaves, Sperber, & Cleaton-Jones, 1990; Carton & Rees, 1987; Cidis, Warshowsky, Goldrich, & Meltzer, 1997; Gedda et al., 1981; Morison, Reyers, & Skorodin, 1994; Newman, Freeman & Holzinger, 1937; Townsend & Richards, 1990; Yager, 1984). Most healthy, non-conjoined twins presumably result from separation of cleavage, morula, or early blastocyst stage embryos

---

FIG. 4. (opposite)   Two specific models for laterality defects in conjoined twins. (A) Schematic of primitive streaks which grow parallel to each other from early stages; this causes right-sided sided *activin* in the left streak to inhibit the normal left-sided expression of *Shh* in the right twin. (B) This would lead to absence of *nodal* expression and thus morphological *situs* defects in the right. When spontaneous chick twins with parallel primitive streaks are examined by *in situ* hybridisation for *Shh* expression, as predicted it is seen that the left twin has normal *Shh* expression (black arrow), but the right twin has a lack of *Shh* expression in the node (white arrows). In contrast, when primitive streaks arise far apart, but grow towards each other during gastrulation, *Shh* expression proceeds normally in both twins (schematised in panel D). However, during head-fold stages, the *Shh* expression of the right twin induces aberrant *nodal* expression on the right side of the left twin (E). When head-fold stage spontaneous chick twins with oblique streaks are examined for *nodal* expression, as predicted it is seen that the right twin has *nodal* expression only on the left side (i.e. normal expression), while the left-most twin has expression (black arrows) on both the left and right sides (which leads to laterality defects, as shown in Levin et al., 1995).

(James, 1983). Thus, some chiral information may be present in the very early mammalian embryo, manifesting itself in hair whorls etc. if the cells are separated at an early stage. In contrast, the asymmetry of the major body organs seems to be unspecified (or at least, plastic enough to be respecified) at those stages, and is developed correctly for both monozygotic twins. This may be related to the fact that heterotaxic reversals in hair whorls and tooth patterns would not be expected to be disadvantageous, whereas discordant *situs* for internal organs clearly is subject to negative evolutionary pressure.

Many interesting questions remain in the field of laterality research. The study of twins, human as well as those of other species, whether conjoined or not, presents unique opportunities to address embryological and evolutionary issues in left–right asymmetry.

Manuscript received and accepted 12 December 1998

REFERENCES

Arey, L. (1965). *Developmental Anatomy*. Philadelphia: Saunders.

Beere, D., Hargreaves, J., Sperber, G., & Cleaton-Jones, P. (1990). Mirror image supplemental primary incisor teeth in twins: Case report and review. *Pediatric Dentistry*, *12*, 390–392.

Burn, J. (1991). Disturbance of morphological laterality in humans. *CIBA Foundation Symposium*, *162*, 282–296.

Carton, A., & Rees, R. (1987). Mirror image dental anomalies in identical twins. *British Dental Journal*, *162*, 193–194.

Cidis, M., Warshowsky, J., Goldrich, S., & Meltzer, C. (1987). Mirror-image optic nerve dysplasia with associated anisometropia in identical twins. *Journal of the American Ptometry Association*, *68*, 325–329.

Collignon, J., Varlet, I., & Robertson, E. (1996). Relationship between asymmetric nodal expression and the direction of embryonic turning. *Nature*, *381*, 155–158.

Fujinaga, M. (1996). Development of sidedness of asymmetric body structures in vertebrates. *International Journal of Developmental Biology*, *41*, 153–186.

Fujinaga, M., & Baden, J.M. (1991). Evidence for an adrenergic mechanism in the control of body asymmetry. *Developmental Biology*, *143*, 203–205.

Gedda, L., Brenci, G., Franceschetti, A., Talone, C., & Ziparo, R. (1981). Study of mirror imaging in twins. *Progress in Clinical and Biological Research*, *69A*, 167–168.

Hoyle, C., Brown, N., & Wolpert, L. (1992). Development of left/right handedness in the chick heart. *Development*, *115*, 1071–1078.

Hummel, K.P., & Chapman, D.B. (1959). Visceral inversion and associated anomalies in the mouse. *Journal of Heredity*, *50*, 9–23.

Hyatt, B., Lohr, J., & Yost, H. (1996). Initiation of left–right axis formation by maternal Vg1. *Nature*, *384*, 62–65.

Hyatt, B.A., & Yost, H.J. (1998). The left–right coordinator: The role of Vg1 in organizing left–right axis. *Cell*, *93*, 37–46.

Isaac, A., Sargent, M.S., & Cooke, J. (1997). Control of vertebrate left–right asymmetry by a snail-related zinc finger gene. *Science*, *275*, 1301.

James, W. (1983). Twinning, handedness, and embryology. *Perceptual and Motor Skills*, *56*, 721–722.

Kapur, R., Jack, R., & Siebert, J. (1994). Diamniotic placentation associated with omphalopagus conjoined twins. *American Journal of Medical Genetics*, *52*, 188–195.

Levin, M. (1997). Left–right asymmetry in vertebrate embryogenesis. *BioEssays*, *19*, 287–296.

Levin, M., Johnson, R.L., Stern, C.D., Kuehn, M.R., & Tabin, C. (1995). A molecular pathway determining left–right asymmetry in chick embryogenesis. *Cell*, *82*, 803–814.

Levin, M., & Mercola, M. (1998a). The compulsion of chirality. *Genes and Development*, *12*, 763–769.

Levin, M., & Mercola, M. (1998b). Events upstream of asymmetrical nodal expression: Reconciling the chick and frog. *Developmental Genetics*, *23*, 185–193.

Levin, M., & Mercola, M. (1998c). Gap junctions are involved in the early generation of left right asymmetry. *Developmental Biology*, *203*, 90–105.

Levin, M., Pagan, S., Roberts, D., Cooke, J., Kuehn, M., & Tabin, C. (1997). Left/right patterning signals and the independent regulation of different aspects of *situs* in the chick embryo. *Developmental Biology*, *189*, 57–67.

Levin, M., Roberts, D., Holmes, L., & Tabin, C. (1996). Laterality defects in conjoined twins. *Nature*, *384*, 321.

Logan, M., Pagán-Westphal, S.M., Smith, D.M., Paganessi, L., & Tabin, C.J. (1998). The transcription factor Pitx2 mediates situs-specific morphogenesis in response to left–right asymmetric signals. *Cell*, *94*, 307–317.

Lowe, L.A., Supp, D.M., Sampath, K., Yokoyama, T., Wright, C.V.E., Potter, S., Overbeek, P., & Kuehn, M.R. (1996). Conserved left–right asymmetry of nodal expression and alterations in murine situs inversus. *Nature*, *381*, 158–161.

Martin-Blanco, E., & Garcia-Bellido, A. (1996). Mutations in the rotated abdomen locus affect muscle development and reveal an intrinsic asymmetry in Drosophila. *Proceedings of the National Academy of Sciences of the United States of America*, *93*, 6048–6052.

Mochizuki, T., Saijoh, Y., Tsuchiya, K., Shirayoshi, Y., Takai, S., Taya, C., Yonekawa, H., Yamada, K., Nihei, H., Nakatsuji, N., Overbeek, P., Hamada, H., & Yokoyama, T. (1998). Cloning of inv, a gene that controls left/right asymmetry and kidney development. *Nature*, *395*, 177–181.

Morison, D., Reyes, C., & Skorodin, M. (1994). Mirror-image tumors in mirror-image twins. *Chest*, *106*, 608–610.

Morrill, C. (1919). Symmetry reversal and mirror imaging in monstrous trout and a comparison with similar conditions in human double monsters. *Anatomical Record*, *16*, 265–292.

Nascone, N., & Mercola, M. (1997). Organizer induction determines left–right asymmetry in *Xenopus. Developmental Biology*, *189*, 68–78.

Newman, H. (1916). Heredity and organic symmetry in armadillo quadruplets. *Biological Bulletin*, *XXX*, 173–203.

Newman, H., Freeman, F., & Holzinger, K. (1937). *Twins: A study of heredity and environment.* Chicago: University of Chicago Press.

Polani, P.E. (1996). Developmental asymmetries in experimental animals. *Neuroscience and Behavioral Reviews*, *20*, 645–649.

Ryan, A.K., Blumberg, B., Rodriguez-Esteban, C., Yonei-Tamura, S., Tamura, K., Tsukui, T., Peña, J.d.l., Sabbagh, W., Greenwald, J., Choe, S., Norris, D., Robertson, E., Evans, R.M., Rosenfeld, M., & Belmonte, J.C.I. (1998). Pitx2 determines left–right asymmetry of internal organs in vertebrates. *Nature*, *394*, 545–551.

Schwind, J. (1934). Symmetry in spontaneous twinning in *Rana sylvatica. Anatomical Record*, *58*, 37.

Spemann, H., & Falkenberg, H. (1919). Über Asymmetrische Entwicklung und Situs inversus viscerum bei Zwillingen und Doppelbildungen. *Wilhelm Roux' Archives Entwicklungsmechanic Organismen*, *45*, 371–422.

Spencer, R. (1992). Conjoined twins: Theoretical embryologic basis. *Teratology*, *45*, 591–602.

Spencer, R. (1995). Rachipagus conjoined twins: They really do occur. *Teratology*, *52*, 346–356.

Supp, D.M., Witte, D., Potter, S., & Brueckner, M. (1997). Mutation of an axonemal dynein affects left–right asymmetry in inversus viscerum mice. *Nature*, *389*, 963–966.

Townsend, G., & Richards, L. (1990). Twins and twinning, dentists and dentistry. *Australian Dental Journal, 35*, 317–327.

Tuinstra, E., DeJong, G., & Scharloo, W. (1990). Lack of response to family selection for directional asymmetry in *Drosophila melanogaster*. *Proceedings of the Royal Society of London Series B, 241*, 146–152.

Winer-Muram, H. (1995). Adult presentation of heterotaxic syndromes and related complexes. *Journal of Thoracic Imaging, 10*, 43–57.

Wood, W. (1997). Left–right asymmetry in animal development. *Annual Review of Cell and Developmental Biology, 13*, 53–82.

Yager, J. (1984). Asymmetry in monozygotic twins. *American Journal of Psychiatry, 141*, 719–720.

Yokoyama, T., Copeland, N.G., Jenkins, N.G., Montgomery, C.A., Elder, F.F., & Overbeek;, P.A. (1993). Reversal of left–right asymmetry: A situs inversus mutation. *Science, 260*, 679–682.

LATERALITY, 1999, *4* (3), 209–255

Symmetry and Asymmetry in the Development of Inner Organs in Parabiotic Twins of Amphibians (Urodela)

Arne von Kraft

*Institute for Anatomy and Cytobiology, Philipps-University,
Marburg, Germany*

Newt embryos of different developmental stages were combined to parabiotic twins in different positions. The exterior appearance and the symmetry relations, particularly of the internal organs (intestinal tract, heart, nuclei habenulae, and vitelline vein) were studied. Experimentally caused organ inversions allowed conclusions with respect to organ asymmetry and unilateral dominance. There was no direct correlation between appearance and symmetry of the exterior and the internal organs. All internal organs showed a continuous transition between normal and ideally inverse situs. The concordance of the organ situs differs greatly. The "left-hand side" or "right-hand side" dominance is not uniform. It depends on the type of fusion, i.e. the relative position of the parabiotic twins, and is often specific for a given organ. In some cases a non-genetic "symmetrisation factor" appears to be strongly active, depending on the fusion type and resulting in a dominant transindividual organ mirror image symmetry in the parabiotic twins. The older twin generally dominates the processes of determination and induction. The "symmetrisation factor" also acts on members of different families, i.e. genetically completely heterogeneous parabiotic twins. The development of organ asymmetry appears to be a process with several phases.

INTRODUCTION

The fundamental form and organisation of vertebrates typically shows a bilateral symmetry, apart from rare exceptions. Some organs, particularly the heart and the gastrointestinal tract, differ from this mirror image symmetry in a constant and regular manner. The heart, primarily an approximately straight tube produced by the combination of bilateral anlagen in amphibians and higher vertebrates, becomes S-shaped: during normal development, the venous part with the sinus venosus and the atrium turns to the left, whereas the ventricle and

Requests for reprints should be sent to Dr Arne von Kraft, In der Goertzbach 43, D-35041 Marburg, Germany

the adjacent bulbus and truncus arteriosus turn to the right. The shape of the heart shows a right-to-left asymmetry in the formation of its regular situs (situs normalis cordis) (see Figs. 6a, $7a_1$ on pp. 219 & 220). The intestine, initially a straight tube, also undergoes an asymmetric transformation during its development: a loop is formed in the duodenal region in combination with a movement of the stomach to the left and of the liver to the right. The pancreas, too, assumes an asymmetric position (Figs. 6a, $7a_1$). Detailed studies of these transformations have been conducted in amphibians. Another situs of regularly occurring asymmetry in these and other organisms, i.e. in cyclostoma and in certain fishes, has been described to involve the nuclei habenulae region of the diencephalon (Fig. 8, p. 223). In addition to these permanently asymmetric situses, the vitelline vein (vena subintestinalis, Figs. 4h, 9, pp. 217 & 224) may transiently assume an asymmetric appearance during the embryonic development of amphibians. The most detailed studies of these organ asymmetries, concerning both morphology and developmental physiology, were performed using the newt *Triturus alpestris* (von Kraft, 1971a, 1976a,b, 1986, 1995a,b, among others; von Woellwarth, 1950; Wehrmaker, 1969).

A variety of classical experimental approaches, which have been complemented by some molecular biological methods during recent years, led to drastic changes of the normal form and laterality (situs normalis or situs solitus) in the asymmetric organs just mentioned. At least in Urodeles it was shown that all kinds of transient forms between the normal situs and the situs inversus can occur, so that a continuous situs spectrum can be achieved (von Kraft, 1968a, 1969b, 1970, 1971b). For different reasons the amphibian embryo was preferred as an experimental model, and most experiments on organ asymmetry and the left–right problem in organogenesis have been performed with these animals (Oppenheimer, 1974). During recent years the intensive molecular biology research into this topic has focused on *Xenopus*, chicken and mouse (for reviews see Levin, 1997; Nascone & Mercola, 1997; Wood, 1997; Yost, 1991, 1995).

In most of the earlier experimental studies it was concluded that the left body side has a general developmental dominance. Based on this dominance of the left-hand side, which was not only observed in amphibians but also in other zoological groups, Corballis and Morgan (1978) postulated a general "gradient hypothesis" of left-sided dominance and applied it to the human situation. This hypothesis was challenged on the basis of experimental results obtained in amphibians and for other reasons by several scientists, including the author of the present review (Corballis & Morgan, 1978/1980, with comments). In a more recent study Morgan (1991, p. 236) continues to discuss a left-to-right gradient in the embryo, emphasising "a more rapid or more extensive development of structures on the *left-hand side* of the body."

My experiments are essentially based on early experiments from Hans Spemann and his co-workers (Fankhauser, 1930; Ruud & Spemann, 1922; Spemann & Falkenberg, 1919): in *Triturus* embryos both artificial monozygotic twins or partial anterior duplications were generated by total or partial ligation. These results made an important contribution to the assumption of left-hand side dominance in the embryo: with 50–83% of organ inversions in the right twin or the right part of the individual, there were partially more inversions in the right part than would be anticipated for a random process. As almost no inversion was observed in the left counterpart of the twins or conjoined twins, this implies the existence of "transindividual" mirror image symmetry of the hearts and/or guts of each partially duplicated individual or pair of twins. I interpret both phenomena taken together ("transindividual" mirror image symmetry and maximal organ inversion) as indicative of an extremely effective process of morphogenetic symmetrisation, leading to a high degree of organ inversion and contrasting the effects produced by mere defects in individual animals. A number of observations demonstrated the dependence of organ symmetry on a chronologically limited process of determination (Oppenheimer, 1974; von Kraft, 1971a), i.e. experimental induction of organ inversion is possible only during a defined developmental phase. Generation of artificial twins (in a broad sense) appeared to be a particularly sensitive system for the study of these phenomena. It is conceivable that a "reciprocal" method of generation of twins by fusion of originally separate, individual embryos to a double organism (parabiotic twins) might lead to new results and far-reaching conclusions (reviewed by von Kraft, 1973). I have used several variations of this method, addressing mainly the following questions:

1. In which form and to what extent are morphological and organ mirror image symmetry present in parabiotic twins?
2. Are organ inversions observed in "left" and "right" parabiotic twins able to support or disprove the hypothesis of left-hand side dominance?
3. Is it possible to elucidate the time course of organ asymmetry determination by the method of parabiotic twin generation?
4. What are the correlations (concordant and discordant) of the asymmetric organs with respect to their situs (see Morgan, 1991; von Kraft, 1971a; Wehrmaker, 1969)?

Important results and aspects from recent molecular biological experiments will be considered later in the Discussion.

MATERIALS AND METHOD

In one series of experiments Axolotl (*Ambystoma mexicanum*) embryos were fused with *Triturus alpestris* embryos in a parabiotic manner. All others studies were performed with *Triturus alpestris* embryos only. Most parabiotic fusion operations used embryos in the neurula stage (N, Harrison-stage 13–22, predominantly 14–16), rarely in the tail-bud stage (S, Harrison-stage 24–27) or the gastrula stage (G, Harrison-stage 9–12c, predominantly 9–11b) (Table 1).

Almost always, embryos of the same age were fused. Exceptions were the lateral fusion of old anterior neurulae with young neurulae (AL-fusion, Fig. 2f) and the fusion of embryos that differed markedly in age (Fig. 2g, Table 1).

The fusion operations on the embryos (Fig. 1, Table 1) were performed under a stereomicroscope in a semi-sterile manner, in wax-filled boxes pretreated with diluted Holtfreter solution containing an antibiotic agent. After the removal of the gelatin coat and the vitelline membrane the embryos were placed in excavations in the wax layer. The regions chosen for fusion were mechanically injured with a fine forceps and the defect regions juxtapositioned. Most embryos fused without complications within hours of the operation and were transferred on the following day as "double embryos" into culture dishes containing dilute

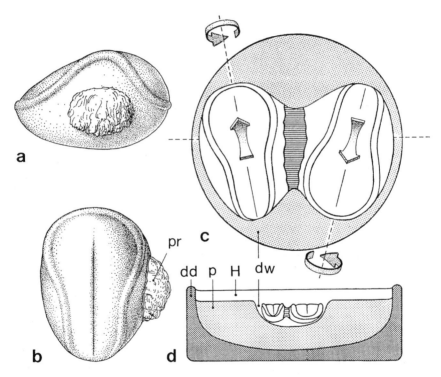

FIG. 1. Schematic representation of a parabiotic experiment, showing the heteropolar fusion of embryos in the neurula stage (He-N, see Fig. 2c). Neurula shown (a) from the right side, (b) from the dorsal side, with hernia-like protrusion of the entodermal layer after injury on the right lateral side (pr). (c) Heteropolarly combined neurulae after right-to-right fusion shown from the dorsal side in the depression well (dw); the area of fusion is shaded. Arrows indicate the embryonic motions in later development (see Fig. 4f and text). (d) Equipment for the operations: Cross-section of a dissection disk (dd) with paraffin-wax layer (p) and Holtfreter solution (H). A parabiotic twin is shown in the enlarged depression well (dw) from the caudal side on the left, and from the rostral side on the right. Enlargement approximately 28fold and twofold in Figs 1a–c and 1d, respectively.

TABLE 1
Modes of Fusion and Labelling of Experimental Groups

Mode of Embryo Fusion	Stage of the Embryos Fused		
	Gastrula (G)	Neurula (N)	Tail-bud stage (S)
Homopolar (Ho) All axes of the body parallel	Ho-G (2e, 4a)	Ho-N (2a, 3b-c) [1] Ho-N/S (2g) Ho-S/N	Ho-S (2h)
Heteropolar (He) Longitudinal axes are opposite	—	[2] He-N-LL He-N-RR (2c)	He-S-LL (4g) He-S-RR
Xenopolar (Xe) Longitudinal and dorso-ventral axes are opposite	—	[3] Xe-N-LD (4e) Xe-N-RD (2b)	—
Dorso-ventral-polar (DV) Dorso-ventral axes are opposite	—	DV-N-LL [2] DV-N-RR (2d, 4c)	—
Dorsal-dorsal (DD) Dorsal-dorsal fusion	—	[4] DD-N (2i, 4d) DD-E	DD-S
Ventral-ventral (VV) Ventral-ventral fusion	—	VV-N (2k, 4h)	—
Anterior-lateral (AL) Fusion of the anterior embryo part with the lateral side	—	[5] AL-N-LA (2f) AL-N-RA (4b)	—

Modes of embryo fusion (parbiose-operation) and overview of the labelling of the experimental groups as used in text, tables, and figures. References to figures are given in brackets. The indices LL, RR, LD, RD, or LA, RA are omitted where they are of no relevance.
[1] N/S and S/N: N-parabiont left (N/S) or right (S/N) respectively.
[2] LL left-left fusion, RR right-right fusion.
[3] LD left embryo, RD right embryo in dorsal positioning.
[4] DD-N neurules of Harrison-stages 14–18 (mostly 14–17).
    DD-E neurules in end-stages (Harrison-stages 19–22).
[5] LA and RA: anterior-part-parabiont with left side (LA) or right side (RA) fused, respectively.

Holtfreter solution with an antibiotic agent, for further development. In order to determine the impact of the surgical procedure and the injury as such on the morphology of the asymmetric organs, individual embryos were injured and cultured in the same manner as the parabiotic twins (defect controls). Normal embryos without injury served as further controls for the statistical analysis of spontaneously occurring inversions. The larvae were cultured until they reached the 3-toe stage when the asymmetry of the studied organs became distinctly visible.

Apart from the overall appearance of the larvae the asymmetric organs, i.e. the intestinal tract, heart, nuclei habenulae of the diencephalon and the vitelline vein system (mainly vena subintestinalis) were examined. The morphology of

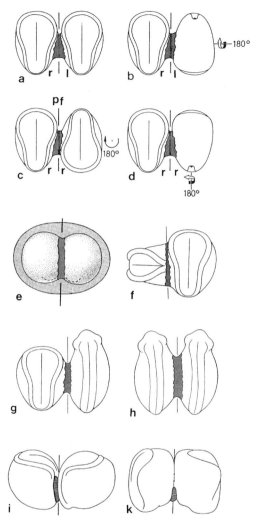

FIG. 2. Schematic representation of the spatial relation of the parabiotic twins as a consequence of different fusion operations: (a) neurulae after homopolar fusion (Ho-N), (b) xenopolar fusion (Xe-N, RD), (c) heteropolar fusion (He-N), and (d) dorsoventral-polar fusion (DV-N). The arrows in b–d indicate the rotation of the embryo necessary for the operation. (e) Gastrulae after hompolar fusion (Ho-G) in the depression well; the curved dashed lines represent the blastopore, which is not visible from the dorsal side. (f) Neurulae after anterior-lateral fusion (AL-N). (g) Neurula after homopolar fusion with a tail-bud embryo (Ho-N/S, Ho-S/N). (h) Tail-bud embryos after homopolar fusion (Ho-S). (i) Neurulae after dorsal-dorsal fusion (DD-N) and (k) after ventral-ventral fusion (VV-N). The plane of fusion is indicated by a vertical straight line, the region of fusion is indicated by the shaded area. (r and l = right-hand side and left-hand side defects, respectively.)

214

the intestinal tract and the heart was judged with a binocular microscope after fixation and removal of the ventral body wall. The symmetric appearance of the nuclei habenulae was judged, if possible, in the same manner after removal of the dorsal skin of the head, or else by microscopic examination of serial sections obtained with standard histological procedures. The vitelline vein system was examined for several days in the living embryo (most non-anaesthetised, in some cases anaesthetised with MS 222). All observations were recorded in detail and documented by photography or artwork.

Statistical analysis of frequency distributions was performed using the χ^2 test. Further details of the quantitative evaluation of morphological results are given in the appropriate results sections.

RESULTS

Exterior Development of Parabiotic twins

A certain percentage of parabiotic embryos die after fusion, but as many as 75–90% of them are available for organ situs analysis during the 3-toe stage in most experimental groups (see following section). The development of the parabiotic larvae followed a normal pattern in the majority of cases. However, abnormal morphogenesis is frequently observed in all experimental groups: hydropsy (ascites, Fig. 3e), malformations of body and tail (Fig. 3e,f), cranial defects and dwarfism of one or both larvae. Dwarfism of one larva only results in attachment of a malformed "parasitic" larva to an almost normally developed larva ("autosite", Fig. 3f). Minimal differences of the parabiotic twins' overall shape, consequently leading to asymmetry, are frequent. However, occasionally a perfect symmetry of the parabiotic twins is observed, particularly impressive in the homopolar group (Ho-N, Fig. 3b–d).

Parabiotic twins of all experimental groups (Ho, He, Xe, DV, DD, see Table 1) tend to approximate or completely fuse their ventral regions (Figs. 3d, 4f,g, 6e,f). In the experimental group DD-N (von Kraft, 1995a), in spite of a dorsal-dorsal fusion of the embryos, in many cases a dorso-ventral polarisation (von Kraft, 1991) of the parabiotic twins occurs: one can distinctly discern a "pair-dorsal side" from a "pair-ventral side", and accordingly a "left" and a "right" parabiont, analogous to the Ho-parabionts (Fig. 4d, Table 1). In addition, a variable tendency to change the polarisation of the (initially opposed) longitudinal axes to a homopolar pattern was observed in the twins fused in a heteropolar manner, also to a lesser extent in twins fused in a xenopolar manner. In extreme cases this secondary rectification was almost perfect (Fig. 4f).

Homopolar arrangement of the embryos frequently either causes reduction or merging of juxtapositional limbs, generating perfectly symmetrical "central extremeties" sometimes characterised by polydactyly (von Kraft, 1976a, 1981; Fig. 5). The process involves fusion of the limb anlagen which undergo symmetrisation, often with concomitant reduction.

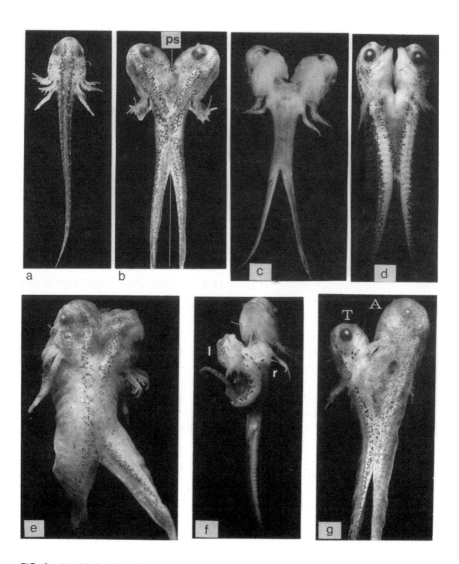

FIG. 3. Parabiotic twins of newts after homopolar fusion (see Fig. 2a,h). (a) Normal individual larva of *Triturus alpestris* in the 3-toe stage. (b)–(c) Parabiotic twins of *Triturus alpestris* after fusion of embryos with perfect exterior symmetry (ps = primary symmetry plane, region of fusion) from the dorsal (b) and the ventral (c) side. (d) Parabiotic twins after fusion of embryos in the tail-bud stage from the dorsal side with concomitant strong ventral convergence. (e) Parabiotic twins with impaired development (hydropsy, malformations of body and tail). (f) Extreme asymmetry of parabiotic twins after fusion of embryos in the tail-bud stage, caused by malformation and dwarfism of the left (l) twin ("parasite"); the right (r) twin has a normal morphologic appearance. (g) Parabiotic twins as seen from the dorsal side after xenoplastic fusion of *Triturus alpestris* (T) and *Ambystoma mexicanum* (A) embryos in the neurula stage. Enlargement approximately 10fold in Fig. 3a–d and (f); 17fold in (e); and 13fold in (g).

216

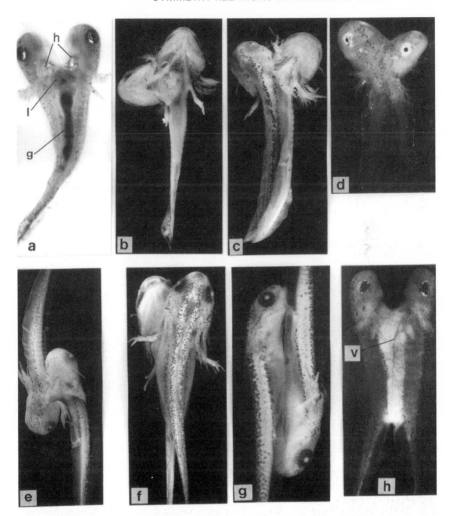

FIG. 4. Parabiotic twins of newts after various types of fusion (see Fig. 2) (a) Ho-G twins as seen from the ventral side (h = heart, l = liver, g = gut); (b) AL-N twins as seen from the ventral side; (c) DV-N twins; (d) DD-N twins as seen from the "dorsal side"; (e) Xe-N twins; (f) He-N twins in extremely homopolar orientation (see arrows in Fig. 1c); (g) He-S twins with completely oppositely oriented body axes, when compared to the initial situation; (h) VV-N twins in an early larva stage with vitelline vein (v). Enlargement ninefold in Fig. 4e, all others approximately 13fold.

It should be noted that there is no association between the overall symmetry of parabiotic twins and the symmetry of their internal organs. A symmetric pair of larvae may exhibit asymmetry of internal organs (asymmetry of the "pair situs", see below), and vice versa, as in the case of the parabiotic twins T 934 (von Kraft, 1973; Ho-S, Figs. 3f and 7k).

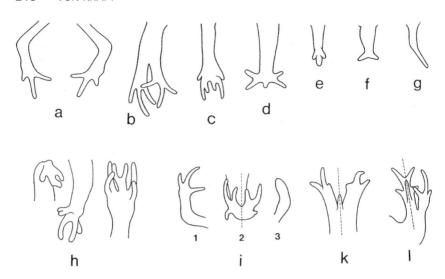

FIG. 5. Development of ''middle extremities'' in parabiotic twins fused in a homopolar manner during their neurula stage (Ho-N). (a) Normal extremities (3-toe stage); the right extremity of the left individual is to be seen on the left side and vice versa. (b)–(g) Various stage of merged extremities, resulting in a single symmetric extremity, and the stepwise reduction thereof in different parabiotic twins. (h) Middle extremities with partial distal duplication of the middle toe, predominantly of symmetric appearance. (i) Approximately symmetric development of the middle extremity (2) combined with completely different lateral extremities characterised by asymmetric appearance to one another, i.e. left extremity of the left twin (1) and right extremity of the right twin (3). (k) and (l) Hypermorphosis of the middle extremity: (k) additional middle toe in the symmetry plane of the basally merged central extremities, (l) perfectly symmetric left extremity of the right twin possessing five toes. The dashed lines in (i) to (l) represent the symmetry planes. Enlargement 18fold in Fig. 5(a)–(g), 27fold in (h), 18fold in (i)–(l).

Development of the Asymmetric Organs

Intestinal Tract and Heart. The optical analysis of morphology and symmetry was carried out either from the ventral side of the parabiotic twins or, if this was prohibited by ventral fusion of various degrees, from the lateral sides (Fig. 7e,f,k,l). A general distinction between a ''pair situs'', i.e. the intestinal and heart situs of the parabiotic twins as a whole (Figs. 6c,d, 7, 8), and an ''individual situs'' (Figs 7, 8) of each of the larvae was made, where possible. If the pair situs could not readily be recognised, e.g. in hetero-and xenopolar parabiotic twins, it was reconstructed from the individual situs analysed from the individual ventral sides (Fig. 7b,c,e,l), using the primary symmetry plane as a reference or mirror image plane. All intermediate stages between a completely normal situs and a perfect situs inversus are possible (Fig. 7a), both in parabiotic twins and in individual larvae. The pair situs of the intestinal tract and the heart show the same behaviour (''Situspektrum''). Accordingly observations are

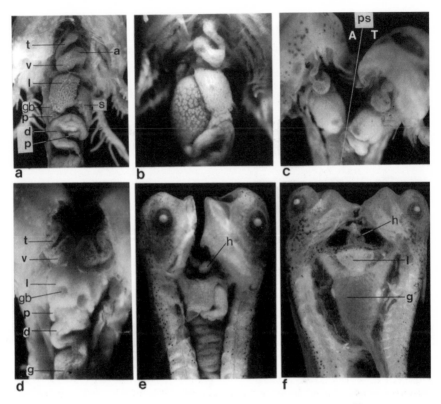

FIG. 6. Organ situs of heart and intestinal tract in individual larvae (a,b) and in parabiotic twins (c–f) as seen from the ventral side (a–d) or from a lateral view (e,f). (a) Normal larva with a typical normal organ situs of heart and intestinal tract. (b) Larva with a perfectly inverse organ situs of heart and intestinal tract. (c) Duplicated Ho-N larva after xenoplastic fusion of an *Ambystoma* (A) with a *Triturus* (T) embryo (see Fig. 3g). Normal organ situs of the heart and normal-median organ situs of the intestinal tract in A, inverse organ situs of the heart and aberrant-median organ situs of the intestinal tract in T (ps = primary symmetry plane). (d) Ho-N parabiotic twins with a normal organ situs of the heart in the right individual (to be seen on the left side of the figure) and an inverse organ situs of the heart in the left individual (to be seen on the right side of the figure). The intestinal tract appears median symmetric, the liver has two gall-bladders. (e) DV-N parabiotic twins with extreme ventral convergence. The hearts of the individuals are separated, showing two normal situses, the intestinal tract has a normal situs. (f) DV-N parabiotic twins showing strong hydropsy and disturbed organ morphogenesis with symmetric appearance. Organ situs diagnosis is not possible. (a = atrium, t = truncus ateriosus, v = ventricle, h = heart, d = duodenum, g = gut, gb = gall-bladder, l = liver, p = pancreas, s = stomach.) Enlargement approximately 28fold in Fig. 6a, 36fold in (b), 20fold in (c), (e) and (f), and 26fold in (d).

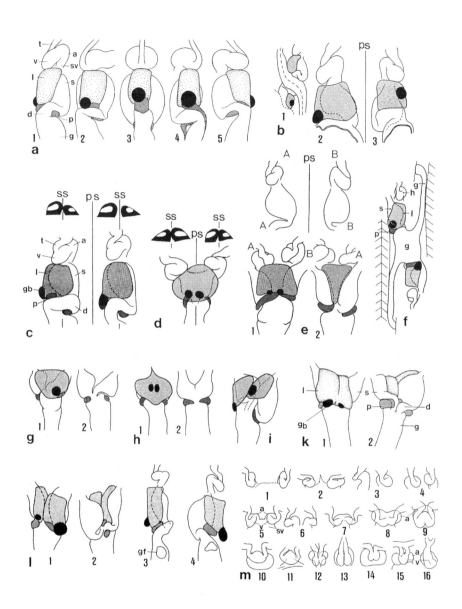

made with respect to pathological organ deformities: all intermediate stages between normal organs (whose situs can readily be analysed) and extremely malformed organs with ill-defined situs escaping analysis are possible. Only those individuals with unequivocally recognisable organ situses were included in the statistical analysis.

The appearance of both paired and individual situs was analysed using the following five distinct classes (Fig. 7a): normal situs (n), normal-median (nm), median or symmetric (m), median-inverse (mi), inverse (i). An "inversion score" (I) was assigned to each of these classes in order to allow quantitative analysis (n = 1, nm = 2, m = 3, mi = 4, i = 5). In an experimental group with completely or predominantly normal organ situs the inversion score will be I = 1 or only slightly higher than 1, respectively. Inversion scores as low as I = 2 indicate a considerable inversion-inducing effect of the experimental operation on the situs of the heart and the intestinal tract. Because the inversions and partial inversions (classes nm, m, mi) of the intestinal tract did not necessarily parallel those of the heart, situs correlations of the asymmetric organs (concordant and discordant) were analysed separately (see later).

FIG. 7 (opposite).   Organ situs of the internal organs in individual larvae (a) and parabiotic twins (b–m) as seen from the ventral side. (a) Situs spectrum of intestinal tract and heart of individual larvae; 1 = normal situs, 2 = normal-median situs, 3 = median (symmetric) situs, 4 = median-inverse situs, 5 = (completely) inverse situs. (b) Xe-N: 1 = intestinal situs as seen from a lateral view. The dashed line indicates the fusion region of the parabiotic twins. 2 and 3 = intestinal organs seen from the ventral side of each individual; organ situs of heart and intestine in 2 are normal, in 3 inverse. (c) DD-N: view from the ventral side of each individual (nuclei habenulae from the dorsal side, above). All organ situses are normal, also the pair situses. (d) Ho-G: strictly median (symmetric) pair situs of all organs, i.e. the left heart organ situs (on the right side of the figure) appears normal, the right heart situs is inverse. The nuclei habenulae exhibit according behaviour (see Fig. 8). (e) VV-N: lateral views of symmetric pair situses, the individual situs in A normal, in B inverse. 1 = "liver side", 2 = "stomach side"; A and B in the upper part of the figure show the view from the ventral side of each individual. (f) He-S: the entire intestinal tract and the heart as seen from a lateral view (liver side) with normal individual situses. (g) Ho-N: organ situs of the intestinal tract appears median-inverse, the liver has been omitted in 2. (h) Ho-N: ideally median pair situs of the intestinal tract. (i) Ho-N: pair situs of the intestinal tract and individual situs have a normal asymmetric appearance. (k) Ho-S (parabiotic twins of Fig. 3f): organ pair situs of the intestinal tract with median (symmetric) appearance, the individual situses of the right twin are normal, on the left-hand side inverse. 1 = view from the "liver side", 2 = view from the "stomach (dorsal) side". (l) Ho-N/S: Median pair situs (1 = lateral view from the "liver side", 2 = lateral view from the "stomach side"). Individual situses (as seen from the individual ventrical side) are normal (3) and inverse (4), respectively. (m) Ho-N: parabiotic twins with median organ pair situs of the heart and various degrees of merging of the heart's anlagen (5–16). a = atrium, d = duodenum, g = gut (intestine), gb = gall-bladder (in black), gf = area of former gut fusion, h = heart, l = liver (lightly shaded), p = pancreas (heavily shaded), ps = primary symmetry plane, ss = secondary symmetry plane, sv = sinus venosus, t = truncus arteriosus, v = ventricle. Enlargement 21fold in Fig. 7a, 11fold in (b₁), 24fold in (b₂₋₃), 22fold in (c) (nuclei habenulae 42fold), 16fold in (d) (nuclei habenulae 46fold), 19fold in (e), 12fold in (f), 16fold in (g), 18fold in (h), 16fold in (i), 19fold in (k), 15fold in (l), and 13fold in (m).

In most cases the assignment of an organ situs to a particular class provided no difficulties. The aforementioned continuous spectrum of organ inversions resulted in a few borderline cases, which had only negligible effects on the statistical analysis.

Nuclei Habenulae.   The nuclei habenulae of the diencephalon, part of the olfactorial system (Kreht, 1939), exhibit an asymmetry with a dominant left-hand side (the left nucleus is considerably larger than the right nucleus, Fig. 8b) in *Triturus alpestris*, but not in all lower vertebrates (Bergquist, 1932). The *Triturus* nuclei habenulae also exhibit a continuous spectrum from normal to inverse organ situses (Fig. 8d). Occasionally, perfectly symmetrical nuclei are found (Fig. 8c).

Both the total size and the size difference between the two nuclei are very variable. They are characterised by a more or less continuous outer layer of heavily staining neuroblasts and a central, only lightly staining fibrous mass. The nuclei habenulae only rarely show structural abnormalities that prohibit the classification of their situs.

As in the analysis of the intestinal tract and heart organ situs, the readily recognisable individual situses were recorded. Because fusions never occurred, the pair situses were obtained by combination of the individual situses (Figs. 7c,d, 8). In contrast with the organ situs of the heart and the intestinal tract, only three classes of nuclei habenulae individual situs were distinguished: normal (n), median (m), and inverse (i) situs. The analysis of the pair situs was carried out according to the five-class system of the heart and the intestinal tract (see previous section).

Intestinal Venous System.   The blood vessels (veins) develop on the ventral side of *Triturus alpestris* during an early larva stage when the extremities are present only as short stumps. The most prominent structure of the vitelline vein system is the vitelline vein itself (vena subintestinalis, Figs. 4h, 9a; von Kraft, 1971b, 1973, 1976b, 1990, 1991, 1995a). The direction of the blood flow in this vessel, which is almost always pointing to the left-hand side of normal individual embryos (normal situs, Fig. 9a), is from caudal to rostral towards the heart. This asymmetry of an organ (in a broad sense) can be recognised from the outside at an early larva stage. By contrast, some of the other asymmetric organs have also entered the phase of morphologic asymmetry during this stage (see Fig. 12), but this is not yet visible from the outside. Both morphogenesis of the vitelline vein and the period of its visibility show great individual variation. Usually it is clearly visible for several days, but in some embryos it may be weakly developed and only transiently visible. If the embryo's overall development is disturbed, the vitelline vein may be completely lacking. In some parabiotic twins no vitelline veins are visible in spite of a normal action of the heart.

A well-developed vitelline vein system initially contains numerous blood vessels (Fig. 9d), but it is subject to constant change. A characteristic feature of

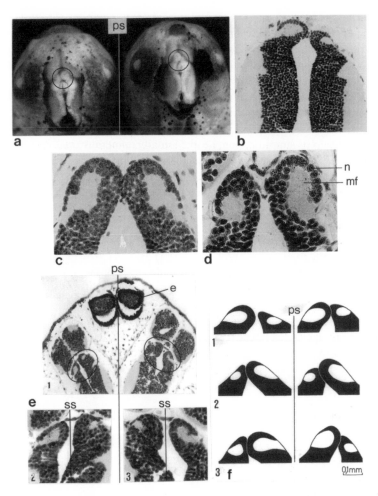

FIG. 8. Symmetry relations of the habenular nuclei of the diencaphalon. (a) Xe-N: symmetric (median) pair situs with an inverse situs on the left-hand side and a normal situs on the right-hand side (region of the nuclei habenulae is encircled, dorsal view. (b) Parabiont with a typical normal situs: the left nucleus is clearly larger than the right one. (c) Exactly median situs of the nuclei habenulae in an individual larva. (d) Parabiont with an inverse situs. (e) Ho-G: parabiotic twins with a symmetric (median) pair situs. 1 = Cross section through the region of the eyes and the diencephalon with the nuclei habenulae (encircled); 2 = normal; 3 = inverse situs. (f) DV-N: schematic representation of the nuclei habenulae organ pair situs in parabiotic twins. 1 = normal asymmetric appearance; 2 = inverse asymmetric appearance; 3 = symmetric appearance. e = eye (cross section), mf = mass of fibres, n = cell nucleus of a neuroblast, ps = primary symmetry plane, ss = secondary symmetry plane. Enlargement 35fold in Fig. 8a, 140fold in (b), 284fold in (c), 331fold in (d), 94fold in (e$_1$), 215fold in (e$_2$) and (e$_3$), 105fold in (f).

its main vessel, the vitelline vein, is its extreme variability at a stage of development in which the other asymmetric organs have already entered the phase of morphologic asymmetry, after they have been asymmetrically determined (see Fig. 12). The variability of the vitelline vein may range to its morphologic inversion, as well as the inversion of the direction of its blood flow (e.g. Fig. 9c,d,g,i). If the situs of the vitelline vein is altered during development, it is more often changed from a primarily inverse situs to a secondarily normal one than vice versa (Fig. 9d,g). The development of the intestinal vein system regularly leads to its simplification, i.e. the initially numerous small and partially interconnected blood vessels are eventually reduced until only the main vessel (vena subintestinalis) is clearly visible. However, sometimes the emergence of more complex structures may be observed.

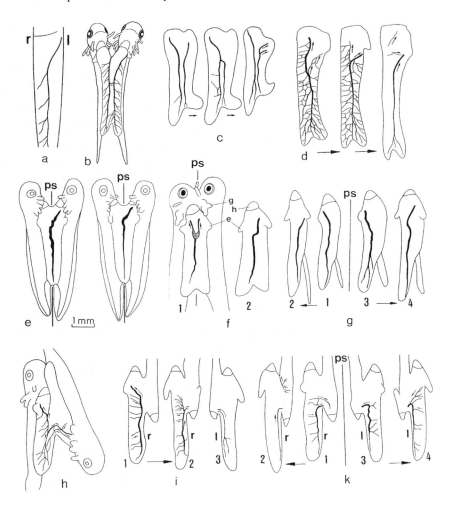

The development of the intestinal vein system of parabiotic twins depends on the fusion type and its developmental consequences, e.g. the extent of ventral convergence. Homopolar fusion of the embryos often leads to the development of two separate vitelline veins (Fig. 9b) which are eventually replaced by a single vessel of regular morphology. Less frequently this fusion type results in the development of only one early vein or transition stages. If ventral convergence of both larvae is prominent, an additional vitelline vein frequently develops on the dorsal side of the organisms, besides the vein on the common ventral side. The ventral fusion of the embryos (VV-N) leads to the development of intestinal veins in each of the "lateral" parts of the pair (Fig. 9e, see also 9g). In the majority of cases these follow the normal direction, i.e. according to the normal situs of the individual larvae in central position. Other types of fusion regularly result in the development of two intestinal veins. In spite of the often complicated growth geometry, an unequivocal assignment of one vein to one of the parabiotic twins is often possible (Fig. 9e–g). The xenopolar type of fusion often results in a situation where the vitelline vein of one of the parabiotic twins is connected to the heart of the other (Fig. 9i,k), making an assignment of the vein to one of the twins impossible. Thus the cardiovascular systems of the parabiotic twins can be interconnected at an early larva stage in a manner that makes an unequivocal separation impossible, just as the hearts of homopolar parabiotic twins or the intestinal tracts may be partially connected (see Fig. 7m).

These classes of situs and direction of the parabiotic twins' intestinal veins are distinguished: normal situs (n, Fig. 9a,b), median situs (m), and inverse situs

---

FIG. 9 (opposite).   Organ situs of the vitelline vein system and its variations, from a ventral view except where indicated otherwise. (a) Individual larva with a normal situs of the vitelline vein pointing to the left-hand side. (b) Ho-S: two vitelline veins with normal situses. (c) Ho-S: development of the vitelline vein system from a combination of normal and inverse (on the left) to an inverse appearance (middle) and back to the original combination with a distal bifurcation (on the right). (d) Ho-N: development of the vitelline vein system from a predominantly inverse appearance (on the left) to a predominantly normal (middle) and entirely normal appearance (on the right). (e) VV-N, lateral view: normal appearance of the vitelline vein. (f) DV-N, lateral view: 1 = bifurcation of the vitelline vein with remnants of the blood island (shaded area); 2 = normal appearance. (g) DV-N, lateral view: organ situs of the vitelline vein on both sides with a primarily inverse appearance (1 and 3) developing into secondary normal situs (2 and 4). (h) Xe-N: inverse (on the left-hand side) and "parabiotic" organ situs of the vitelline vein. (i) Xe-N: development of the vitelline vein organ situs of the parabiotic twin on the right-hand side (r) from inverse (1) to "parabiotic" (2) within three days, with concomitant symmetric-"parabiotic" appearance of the vitelline vein (3) of the twin on the left-hand side (l). (k) Xe-N: vitelline veins of both parabiotic twins have a primarily "parabiotic" appearance (1 and 3) which does not alter during the later stages of development (2 and 4). Arrows indicate the direction of blood flow. Only the main vessels are shown in most cases. e = limb (extremity) bud, g = gill anlage, h = area of the heart, l = left parabiotic twin, r = right parabiotic twin, ps = primary symmetry plane, identifcal to the primary region of fusion in (e) and to the secondary region of fusion in (f). Enlargement 18fold in Fig. 9a, 10fold in (b), approximately 13fold in (c), 12fold in (d), 11fold in (e)–(k).

(i, Fig. 9c middle, $g_{1,3}$). Median situs occur only rarely and transiently. Intermediate stages between these classes are possible, as with the intestinal tracts, hearts and nuclei habenulae (see later for the correlation of intestinal vein, intestinal tract, and heart).

Individual Situses of the Asymmetric Organs and "Unilateral Dominance". Control larvae of *Triturus alpestris* only rarely exhibit a deviation from the normal situs; accordingly, their inversion score is only slightly above 1 (Table 2). A lateral injury to the embryo without subsequent fusion has a significant effect on the frequency of partial and total organ inversions (Defect controls, Table 2). Nevertheless, a comparison of the frequency of organ inversions of "defect controls" and parabiotic embryos (e.g. the Ho-N experimental group) shows that the increased number of inversions in the Ho-N group cannot be interpreted as a mere consequence of injury, but is rather a specific effect caused by the parabiotic fusion of the embryos at the neurula stage. The differences are statistically highly significant in nearly all cases.

In general, the type of parabiotic fusion in the experimental groups has a great influence on the frequency of organ inversions, as clearly expressed in the inversion scores, e.g. the extremely high inversion scores of the DD-N group (Table 2) as opposed to the generally much lower scores of the DV-N group (Table 3) or the scores of the VV-N group (data not shown). On average the frequency of inversions is much higher in the groups of heterolaterally fused embryos (right-hand to left-hand side fusion, Ho-and Xe-parabiotic twins) and in the DD-N group on the one hand, than in the groups of homolaterally fused embryos (right-to-right and left-to-left fusions, He-N and DV-N; Table 3) and the VV-N group on the other. The fusion geometry thus has a great influence on the extent of alteration of the organ situses.

The age at which the fusion of the embryos is performed is also of crucial importance for the occurrence of organ inversions, as shown by the inversion scores of the Ho-N $L > R$ and $R < L$ groups (Table 2). The inversion scores of the older one of the parabiotic twins are rather low when compared to the extremely high inversion scores of the younger one of the parabiotic twins. Accordingly, the comparison of the Ho-N and Ho-S groups shows a striking decrease of the inversion scores with increasing age of the fused embryos. The age dependence of the induction of organ inversions is further indirectly demonstrated by the data presented in Table 5 for the DD-N, DD-E, and DD-S groups (see later). The inversion scores of the (older) anterior parabiotic twins in the Al-LA and -RA groups (Table 3) are statistically significantly lower than the scores for the (younger) complete parabiotic twin, with one exception. Parabiotic fusion has a strong influence on organ asymmetry during the gastrula (Ho-G, Table 2) and neurula (Ho-N) stages of embryonic development, with a decreasing tendency during the neurula stage. The possibility of influencing organ asymmetries is lost during the tail-bud stage of embryonic development (Ho-S, Table 2). According to Tables 2 and 3 the inversion frequencies of the various asymmetric organs are in part strikingly different (see later).

Is there any "unilateral dominance" of the *Triturus alpestris* embryo with respect to asymmetry (or generation of a normal situs) which could be demonstrated by the parabiotic fusion experiments presented here? A definition of "left-hand" or "right-hand" side dominance appears to be necessary. In a pair of parabiotic twins, the (left or right) individual whose organs predominantly exhibit the original organ situs, i.e. the morphologically normal situs, as opposed to the more strongly inverse partner is regarded as the dominant one. In parabiotic twins generated by homolateral or one-sided asymmetric fusion (Table 3) the side with less frequently altered organ situs is to be regarded as dominant. "Dominance" with respect to organ asymmetry is defined as the relatively or absolutely predominant generation of a normal situs (see Discussion). The results are summarised in Table 4. There appears to be a "mosaic" of various unilateral dominances, differing in part between one experimental group and the other with respect to an individual organ, as well as between one organ and the other within one experimental group. A large degree of variation is found even within one experimental group or fusion type (e.g. Table 4, Ho-G and Ho-N, heart), pointing to a change of dominance during development. It must be concluded that the experiments conducted with parabiotic twins not only do not support the concept of embryonic or organ asymmetry as a determining factor of development in general, but actually contradict such a concept.

Three single observations should be noted. (a) In all cases there was a strong correlation of dominance with respect to the heart and the vitelline vein (see also later). (b) Backward arrangement of an embryo leads to a clear tendency towards organ inversions in the xenopolar type of fusion. (c) There is a strong left-hand side dominance of the nuclei habenulae in the Ho-N and Ho-G groups, particularly strong in the latter (Tables 2 and 4): the left-hand sided position of an embryo as such results in a strongly predominant generation of normal situs (two out of three cases in the Ho-G group), whereas the right-hand sided position results in a predominant generation of mirror-inverse situs (60% of all cases in the Ho-G group).

Organ Symmetrisation and "Pair Situs".   The "pair situs" is an indicator of the overall symmetric or asymmetric arrangement of organs (or pairs of organs, respectively) in parabiotic twins. Organ-pair situses of parabiotic twins are frequently symmetric. In some experimental groups this symmetric arrangement, and not the partially symmetric or asymmetric arrangement, is the predominant type (Table 5). There is a general correlation of the frequency of inversion or the inversion score of an organ (including the vitelline vein) on the one hand and the frequency of a symmetric pair situs on the other. Apparently the generation of a symmetrical pair situs is linked to the possibility of the generation of an inverse asymmetric organ situs (see Figs. 7b,d,e,h,k,l, 8a,e, 9k). This results in observations like those discussed earlier:

TABLE 2
Organ Situs in the Experimental Groups

Experimental Group	Organ		Group Size n	normal + normal-median n	%	median n	%	median-inverse + inverse n	%	I	P-score	
Controls	Int. tr.		103	97	94	3	3	3	3	1,2	a₁	
	Heart		105	103	98	1	1	1	1	1,1	a₂	
	Haben.		98	95	97	3	3	0	0	1,1	a₃	
Defect controls	Int. tr.		214	150	70	24	12	40	19	2,0	a₁<0.001	
	Heart		212	158	75	12	6	42	20	1,9	a₂<0.001	
	Haben.		210	142	68	36	18	32	15	2,0	a₃<0.001	
Ho-S	Int. tr.		84	80	95	2	2	2	2	1,1	—	
	Heart		79	77	97	0	0	2	3	1,1	—	
	Haben.		84	82	98	1	1	1	1	1,1	—	
Ho-N L=R	Heart	le	56	23	41	14	25	19	34	2,8	>0.05	a₂D<0.001
		ri	56	35	62	9	16	12	21	2,2		a₂D<0.05
	Haben.	le	77	56	73	7	9	14	18	1,9		a₃D>0.05
		ri	77	37	48	12	16	28	36	2,8	<0.01	a₃D<0.001
L>R	Heart	le	43	33	77	3	7	7	16	1,8	—	
		ri	43	18	42	1	2	24	56	3,2	a₂D<0.001	
	Haben.	le	87	75	86	3	3	9	10	1,5	—	
		ri	87	24	28	23	26	40	46	3,4	a₃D<0.001	
R>L	Heart	le	82	8	10	15	18	59	72	4,2	a₂D<0.001	
		ri	82	74	90	8	10	0	0	1,2	—	
	Haben.	le	107	21	20	11	10	75	70	4,0	a₃D<0.001	
		ri	107	81	76	15	14	11	10	1,6	—	

Group	Organ	Side								I	P
DD-N	Heart	le	52	15	29	9	17	28	54	3,3	<0.05
		ri	52	24	46	13	25	15	29	2,6	
	Haben.	le	40	16	40	3	8	21	52	3,3	<0.05
		ri	40	27	67	2	5	11	28	2,2	
	Vit. v.	le	9	2	22	0	0	7	78	4,1	<0.05*
		ri	9	7	78	1	11	1	11	1,7	
Ho-G	Int. tr.	le	20	11	55	4	20	5	25	2,5	>0.05
		ri	23	9	39	6	26	8	35	2,8	
	Heart	le	49	30	61	5	10	14	29	2,4	<0.05
		ri	50	18	36	5	10	27	54	3,3	
	Haben.	le	120	79	66	19	16	22	18	2,0	<0.001
		ri	119	27	23	20	17	72	60	3,8	
Xe-N, LD	Int. tr.	le	64	6	9	28	44	30	47	3,5	<0.001
		ri	64	54	84	9	14	1	2	1,6	
	Heart	le	84	58	69	16	19	10	12	2,1	<0.01
		ri	75	37	49	14	19	24	32	2,6	
	Haben.	le	49	11	22	9	18	29	59	3,7	<0.00
		ri	48	36	75	4	8	8	17	1,8	
	Vit. v.	le	27	23	85	0	0	4	15	1,6	1<0.02
		ri	37	12	32	0	0	25	68	3,7	
RD	Int. tr.	le	34	2	6	14	41	18	53	3,8	<0.001
		ri	34	23	68	8	23	3	9	1,9	
	Heart	le	143	85	59	31	22	27	19	2,3	<0.001
		ri	148	37	25	14	9	97	66	3,7	
	Haben.	le	31	7	23	3	10	21	68	3,9	>0.05
		ri	30	11	37	6	20	13	43	3,1	
	Vit. v.	le	41	35	85	0	0	6	15	1,6	<0.001
		ri	35	5	14	0	0	30	86	4,4	

Organ situs situations on the left-hand side and right-hand side in various experimental groups of parabiotic twins. Haben. = habenular nuclei, Int. tr. = intestinal tract, Vit. v. = vitelline vein, I = inversion score, ri = right, le = left, > = older than (Experimental group). For the comparison of P-values, the groups of parabiotic twins were named with an identical symbol—a_1, a_1, etc., D (a_2D) etc.—as the respective defect controls. See text for more details. *calculated by Fischer's test. See text for more details. See also Table 1.

TABLE 3

Organ Situs Situations in Various Groups of Parabiotic Twins after Homolateral Fusion or of Markedly Different Developmental Age at Time of Fusion

Experimental Group	Organ	Group Size n	Organ Situs								
			normal + normal-median		median		median-inverse + inverse		I	P-score
			n	%	n	%	n	%		
He-N LL	Int. tr.	143	131	92	11	8	1	1	1,3	$a_1 < 0.001$
	Heart	158	95	60	19	12	44	28	2,3	$a_2 < 0.001$
	Haben.	191	164	86	8	4	19	10	1,5	$a_3 < 0.001$
RR	Int. tr.	150	25	17	36	24	89	59	3,6	a_1
	Heart	191	126	66	40	21	25	13	2,0	a_2
	Haben.	219	119	54	18	8	82	37	2,7	a_3
DV-N LL	Int. tr	77	54	70	18	23	5	6	1,8	$b_1 > 0.05$
	Heart	212	132	62	27	13	53	25	2,2	$b_2 < 0.001$
	Haben.	284	166	58	38	13	80	28	2,4	$b_3 < 0.001$
	Vit. v.	129	84	65	5	4	40	31	2,3	$b_4 < 0.001$
RR	Int. tr	84	63	75	10	12	11	13	1,8	b_1
	Heart	192	147	77	22	11	23	12	2,0	b_2
	Haben.	272	221	81	21	8	30	11	1,6	b_3
	Vit. v.	103	86	83	12	12	5	5	1,4	b_4

TABLE 3 (Continued)

Experimental Group	Organ	Group Size n	normal + normal-median n	normal + normal-median %	median n	median %	median-inverse + inverse n	median-inverse + inverse %	I	P-score
Ho – N/S	Int. tr.	72	30	42	20	28	22	31	2,8	$c_1 < 0.001$
	Heart	79	45	57	23	29	11	14	2,2	$c_2 < 0.002$
	Haben.	84	59	70	10	12	15	18	2,0	$c_3 < 0.001$
S/N	Int. tr.	63	52	83	10	16	1	2	1,6	c_1
	Heart	63	23	37	14	22	26	41	2,9	c_2
	Haben.	75	31	41	9	12	35	47	3,1	c_3
AL – LA	Int. tr.	57	43	75	11	19	3	5	1,8	$d_1 < 0.001$
	Heart	86	36	42	17	20	33	38	2,9	$d_2 > 0.05$
	Haben.	85	37	44	16	19	32	38	2,9	$d_3 > 0.05$
RA	Int. tr.	54	7	13	16	30	31	57	3,6	d_1
	Heart	69	34	49	17	24	18	26	2,6	d_2
	Haben.	70	22	31	10	14	38	54	3,5	d_3

For abbreviations see footnote to Table 2. See text for more details. See also Tables 1 and 2.

TABLE 4

Unilateral Dominance of the Asymmetric Organs in Various Groups of Parabiotic Twins

Experimental Group	Organs			
	Intestinal Tract	Heart	Habenular Nuclei	Vitelline Vein
Ho-G	le (>0.05)	le (<0.05)	le (<0.001)	—
Ho-N L=R)	—	ri (>0.05)	le (<0.01)	—
DD-N	—	ri (<0.05)	ri (<0.05)	ri (<0.05)
Xe-N LD	ri (<0.001)	le (<0.01)	ri (<0.001)	le (<0.02)
RD	ri (<0.001)	le (<0.001)	ri (>0.05)	le (<0.001)
Ho-N/S, S/N	"le" (<0.001)	"ri" (<0.002)	"ri" (<0.001)	—
AL – LA	"le" (<0.001)	"ri" (>0.05)	"le" (>0.05)	—
He-N LL, RR	"le" (<0.001)	"ri" (<0.001)	"le" (<0.001)	—
DV-N LL, RR	le = ri	"ri" (<0.001)	"ri" (<0.001)	"ri" (<0.001)

le = left, ri = right dominance. See text for more details. See also Table 1.

1. The frequency of symmetric pair situs decreases with the age of the embryos, e.g. predominant formation of symmetric pair situs is observed in the DD-N group, whereas only asymmetric pair situses are found in the DD-S group (Table 5).

2. The frequency of symmetric pair situs strongly depends on the type of embryonic fusion: heterolaterally fused parabiotic twins (Ho-G, Ho-N, Xe-N) as well as DD-N duplicated organisms exhibit an extremely strong dominance of symmetry. Homolateral fusions (He-N, DV-N) result in predominantly asymmetric paired organ situs. In part this is also true for the VV-N group. In some experimental groups (e.g. Xe-N) there are significantly different frequencies of symmetry depending on the type of fusion (e.g. RD and LD; Table 5).

3. As with the individual situs and the situs inversions, clear differences were also observed with respect to the symmetry of the pair situs; however they did not seem to follow a general rule or pattern.

As noted earlier, there is no direct correlation of the overall exterior symmetry of a pair of parabiotic twins and the symmetry of its internal organs. They may be completely different (see "Exterior Development"). The almost complete dominance of symmetric organ pair situs (Table 5) in spite of the fusion-induced asymmetry of the overall exterior shape (Figs. 2b, 4e), as observed in parabiotic twins fused in a xenopolar manner (Xe-N), is particularly noteworthy. The developmental process causing organ symmetrisation is obviously not dependent on or linked to the symmetry pattern of the parabiotic twins' overall exterior appearance.

Homopolar "xenoplastic" fusion of embryos in the neurula stage belonging to different species of Urodelae such as *Triturus alpestris* and *Ambystoma mexicanum* also resulted in organ inversions and, consequently, in mirror-symmetrical organ pair situses, just as with intraspecific *Triturus* parabiotic twins (von Kraft, 1985). This was observed with all organs and with equal of even increased frequency (Table 5). The symmetrisation processes are apparently of a trans-specific nature (see Discussion). In spite of the small number of xenoplastic *Triturus/Ambystoma*-Ho-N parabiotic twins, a high statistical significance is obtained (Table 5) if the *Triturus/Triturus* Ho-S group is used as a control (*Triturus/Ambystoma* Ho-S was not determined).

Organ Situs Correlations.   In general the asymmetric organs exhibit a tendency towards concordant situs. In individual organisms or in parabiotic twins with low inversion scores this concordance is strongly or completely dominant, e.g. in the He-S groups (Table 6). With increasing frequency of partial and complete organ inversions this concordance becomes weaker (e.g. He-N groups), i.e. the individual organs' situses differ to a variable degree, the most extreme example being the He-N RR group. A strong tendency to inversion is apparently related to an "independent" behaviour of the individual organ situs with respect to the asymmetric form of the total organism. All conceivable organ situs combinations, including completely oppositely directed organ situs, are indeed found if sufficient numbers of strongly inverse parabiotic twins are studied. This can be indirectly concluded from the results obtained with the individual and pair situs whose obvious divergence is a consequence of the situs-discordance of the involved organs. The concordance based on the pair situs is generally higher than that based on the individual situs.

Obvious differences with respect to the situs correlations are not only found between experimental groups with a different type of fusion, but also within such groups if the geometry is different (e.g. He-N and Xe-N groups in Table 6). In the Xe-N groups the situs concordance is considerably influenced by right, left normal (ventral), or opposite (dorsal) positioning of an individual. Thus both the lateral position and the position of the embryo in the dorsoventral axis have a strong influence on the situs correlations. The fusion type of the parabiotic twins not only influences the organs' inversion frequencies but also their situs concordance.

In complete agreement with the results obtained for the individual situs, a stronger correlation of the situs concordance of heart and vitelline vein is found when compared to that of the vitelline vein and the intestinal tract (e.g. Xe-N groups, Table 6).

TABLE 5
Symmetry Relations

Experimental Group	Organ	Group Size n	Asym. n	Asym. %	Partial Sym. n	Partial Sym. %	Sym. (m) n	Sym. (m) %	I	P-score
Ho-G	Int. tr.	69	10/0	14	10/5	22	44	64	2,6	
	Heart	90	26/8	38	12/9	23	35	39	2,6	
	Haben.	93	16/9	28	9/12	22	47	51	2,9	
Ho-N	Int. tr	245	30/0	12	77/12	36	126	51	2,5	
	Heart	263	48/3	19	61/15	29	136	52	2,5	
	Haben.	271	45/5	18	50/13	23	158	58	2,6	
Ho-S	Int. tr.	42	39/0	93	2/0	5	1	2	1,1	f_1
	Heart	38	35/0	92	1/0	3	2	5	1,1	f_2
	Haben.	42	40/0	95	1/0	2	1	2	1,1	f_3
DD-N	Int. tr.	32	1/0	3	8/1	28	22	69	2,7	$a_1 < 0.001 \ c_1$
	Heart	138	4/5	6	28/20	35	81	59	3,0	$a_2 < 0.001 \ c_2$
	Haben.	118	19/4	19	20/6	15	77	65	2,7	$a_3 < 0.001 \ c_3$
	Vit. v.	79	1/0	8	1/0	8	10	83	2,7	
DD-E	Int. tr	97	42/0	43	37/1	39	17	18	1,8	$a_1 \ b_1 < 0.005$
	Heart	110	41/0	37	33/7	36	29	26	2,0	$a_2 \ b_2 < 0.001$
	Haben.	86	63/0	73	8/0	9	15	18	1,4	$a_3 \ b_3 < 0.005$
	Vit. v.	62	37/1	61	3/2	8	19	31	1,8	
DD-S	Int. tr.	115	93/0	81	17/0	15	5	4	1,2	b_1
	Heart	121	103/0	85	16/0	13	2	2	1,2	b_2
	Haben.	95	88/0	93	4/0	4	3	3	1,1	b_3
	Vit. v.	56	50/0	89	2/0	4	4	7	1,2	

TABLE 5 (Continued)

			Organ Situs								
		Group Size	Asym.		Partial Sym.		Sym. (m)				
Experimental Group	Organ	n	n	%	n	%	n	%	I	P-score	
VV-N	Int. tr.	79	22/2	30	15/7	28	33	42	2,4	$c_1 < 0.005$	
	Heart	82	30/2	39	18/5	28	27	33	2,2	$c_2 < 0.001$	
	Haben.	122	54/6	49	12/5	14	45	37	2,2	$c_3 < 0.001$	
	Vit. v.	49	33/4	76	3/1	8	8	16	1,8		
Xe-N RD	Int. tr.	80	7/2	11	24/6	38	41	51	2,7	$d_1 > 0.05$	
	Heart	242	16/23	16	44/46	37	113	47	3,1	$d_2 < 0.001$	
	Haben.	199	15/31	23	13/46	30	94	47	3,3	$d_3 > 0.05$	
Xe-N LD	Int. tr.	69	5/0	7	28/4	46	32	46	2,5	d_1	
	Heart	174	51/1	30	66/13	45	43	25	2,1	d_2	
	Haben.	174	25/12	21	37/17	31	83	48	2,7	d_3	
He-N RR	Int. tr.	56	2/7	16	8/28	64	11	20	3,5	$e_1 < 0.001$	
	Heart	81	38/5	53	23/5	35	10	12	2,0	$e_2 > 0.05$	
	Haben.	99	34/16	51	5/5	10	39	39	2,6	$e_3 < 0.001$	
He-N LL	Int. tr.	58	39/0	67	19/0	33	0	0	1,3	e_1	
	Heart	64	27/5	50	14/8	34	10	16	2,2	e_2	
	Haben.	85	64/2	78	6/1	8	12	14	1,5	e_3	
Triturus/Ambystoma	Int. tr.	13	1/1	15	4/0	31	7	54	2,7	$f_1 < 0.001$	
Ho-N	Heart	24	5/0	21	4/0	17	15	62	2,4	$f_2 < 0.001$	
	Haben.	8	0/0	0	1/0	12	7	87	2,9	$f_3 < 0.001$	

Symmetry relations of the pair situses in various groups of parabiotic twins. Asymmetry = normal (n) and inverse (i) pair situses; partial symmetry = normal-median (nm) and median-inverse (mi) pair situses; symmetry = median (m) pair situs. I = inversion score. For the calculation and comparison of P values see footnote to Table 2. See text for more details. See also Table 1.

TABLE 6
Situs Correlations

Experimental Group	Organ Comparison	Group Size n	Situs Concordance					
			Unequivocal		Almost concordant		Absent	
			n	%	n	%	n	%
He-S LL ind. s.	Int. tr.-Heart	71	60	84	7	10	4	6 (0)
''	Int. tr.-Haben.	67	56	84	4	6	7	10 (7)
''	Heart-Haben.	68	58	85	2	3	8	12 (3)
He-S RR	Int. tr.-Heart	119	98	82	11	9	9	8 (0)
''	Int. tr.-Haben.	109	93	85	8	7	8	7 (1)
''	Heart-Haben.	111	105	95	0	0	6	5 (0)
He-N LL	Int. tr.-Heart	129	78	60	17	13	34	26 (16)
''	Int. tr.-Haben.	135	95	70	20	15	20	15 (7)
''	Heart-Haben.	146	87	60	14	10	45	31 (23)
He-N RR	Int. tr.-Heart	144	29	20	42	29	65	51 (35)
''	Int. tr.-Haben.	143	34	24	34	24	75	52 (41)
''	Heart-Haben.	178	84	47	19	11	75	42 (32)
He-N LL pair s.	Int. tr.-Heart	50	32	64	8	16	10	20
''	Int. tr.-Haben.	52	39	75	13	25	0	0
''	Heart-Haben.	53	26	49	18	34	9	17
He-N RR	Int. tr.-Heart	53	12	23	16	30	25	47
''	Int. tr.-Haben.	52	16	31	20	38	16	31
''	Heart-Haben	73	27	37	24	33	22	30

TABLE 6 (Continued)

Experimental Group		Organ Comparison	Group Size n	Situs Concordance					
				Unequivocal		Almost concordant		Absent	
				n	%	n	%	n	%
Ho-N	"	Intr. tr.-Heart	222	108	49	83	37	31	14
(total)	"	Int. tr.-Haben.	197	91	46	80	41	26	13
	"	Heart-Haben.	212	114	54	63	30	35	16
Xe-N LD indiv. s.		Int. tr.-Vit.v.	29	10	34	—	—	19	66
	"	Heart-Vit.v.	45	33	73	—	—	12	27
Xe-N RD	"	Int. tr.-Vit.v.	29	5	17	—	—	24	83
	"	Heart-Vit.v.	43	24	56	—	—	19	44

Correlations of the organ situses in various groups of parabiotic twins. Situses are regarded as "unequivocally concordant" if the difference of situs classes (SD) = 0; and as "almost concordant" if the SD = 1 (e.g. n/nm, m/mi). Concordance is regarded as "absent" if SD = 2–4 (e.g. n/m, nm/i etc.). Numbers in parentheses indicate organ situses with completely opposite orientation (SD 3–4). Due to the lack of median vitelline veins in the Xe-N group, slight differences of the organ situs (SD = 1) were regarded as "unequivocal". ind.s. = individual situs, pair.s. = pair situs. For abbreviations see footnote to Table 2. See text for more details. See also Table 1.

237

CONCLUSIONS AND DISCUSSION OF RESULTS

Aspects of "Transindividual" Organ Symmetry

The parabiotic experiments conducted here continue Spemann's earlier work with artificial partial duplications and twins of *Triturus* (see Introduction), but with reverse methodology, i.e. the generation of artificially duplicated organisms from primarily individual ones. As Spemann had already noted, the right half of the embryo becomes the mirror image of the left; the frequently observed inversions in the right parabiotic twin are interpreted as a consequence of a still unknown process causing organ symmetrisation (Spemann & Falkenberg, 1919, p.406). In an earlier publication (von Kraft, 1976b, Fig. 10)

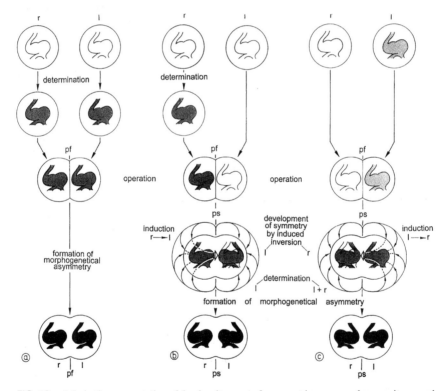

FIG. 10. Schematic representation of the development of asymmetric organs and organ situses and development of transindividual organ mirror image symmetry with Ho-S (a) and Ho-N parabiotic twins (b) and (c). The development of the heart is used as an example for the various stages of determination at the time of the operation. Open symbol = anlage in the predetermination phase; lightly shaded symbol in (c) = reversibly determined anlage; heavily shaded symbol = irreversibly determined anlage; closed symbol = morphologically manifest heart shape of the larva at a later stage. "r" and "l" refer to the right and left parabiotic twin, respectively. pf = plane of fusion, ps = primary symmetry plane. See text for more details.

I have developed a concept of a developmental system generating transindividual mirror image symmetry in pairs of organs, rather than interpreting such symmetry as a consequence of a defect only. The experiments reported here were meant to elucidate the fundamental question whether transindividual mirror image symmetry can be generated only by division of an individual embryo, or whether it can also be generated by artificial fusion of two separate individuals, as with the parabiotic twins. The results are obviously in favour of the latter possibility. The dominance of symmetrical organ pair situs is obviously not merely the consequence of a defect (defect controls in Table 2 and Table 5). The results rather suggest a "symmetrisation factor" of its own, just like the results of Spemann's earlier ligation experiments. This symmetrisation factor is for the present defined in a purely descriptive manner as a developmental process acting on both embryos, causing regular or (partially) inverse development of the embryos' anlagen depending on the fusion type and the age of the embryos at which the fusion was performed. A typical process of determination, as defined by the classical developmental biology (see later), is combined with a process of induction. In general the older parabiotic twin is also the more strongly determined, and consequently develops regular organ situs, whereas the younger, less strongly determined parabiotic twin displays more or less inversion. The older parabiotic twin thus functions as an "inducer", which causes organ inversion in the less determined "reactive" twin. In this manner the parabiotic twins may be interpreted as an induction system in which the more strongly determined embryo, acting as an "active system" under the influence of the transindividual symmetrisation factor, produces an organ situs inversion in the "reactive system", i.e. the less strongly determined embryo (von Kraft 1976b; Fig. 10).

The reference plane of organ mirror image symmetry and of the symmetrisation processes is the main or primary symmetry plane of the parabiotic twins, which is identical to the fusion plane in those embryos that were fused in a homopolar manner (see Fig. 2a), but must be constructed in other fusion types by rotation of one of the parabiotic twins until a position analogous to a homopolar position is reached (Figs. 2b–d). It should be noted that the symmetrisation processes involving the internal organs are completely independent of the exterior body symmetry. This effect could be observed in the Ho-groups and, even more clearly, in the Xe-groups. Apparently, there is a special interrelation of the organ anlagen (morphogenetic fields) of intestinal tract, heart, and nuclei habenulae of those parabiotic twins that were fused in a xenopolar manner unrelated to the overall exterior appearance and its asymmetry (Fig. 11).

As already noted, the process of symmetrisation depends on the age and state of determination of the parabiotic twins on the one hand, and on their spatial relation on the other. Heterolateral, i.e. left-to-right or dorso-dorsal fusion of the embryos appears to be a prerequisite for optimal symmetrisation of a paired

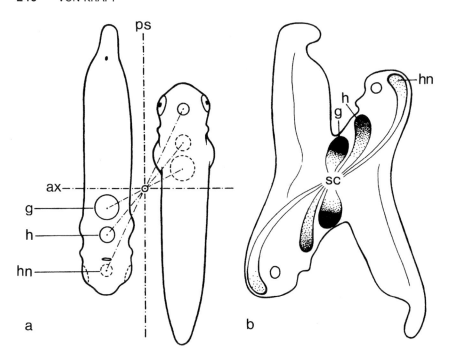

FIG. 11.   Relation of position and symmetry of parabiotic twins after xenopolar fusion (Xe-N) and their regions of organ anlagen. Intestinal tract (gut, g), heart (h), and habenular nuclei (hn) at the beginning of the experiment (a) and after fusion with marked "ventral convergence" (b) (schematic representation). For the sake of clarity of the organ regions and their common centre of symmetry (sc) juvenile larvae rather than embryos at the neurula stage were depicted in (a) (left in ventral view, right in dorsal view). The dashed lines connecting the respective organ anlagen are to be imagined as inclined with respect to the paper plane (experimental combination LU). The parabiotic twins are dislocated along an axis parallel to their primary symmetry plane (ps). The centre of symmetry is defined by the intersection of the primary symmetry plane and the axis of rotation (ax). The spatial relation of the corresponding organ areas in (b) is emphasised with respect to the centre of symmetry (sc). See text for more details.

organ situs. Homolateral fusion (left-to-left or right-to-right connection, von Kraft, 1980, 1991) generally has a much weaker inverting, and thus symmetry-producing influence (He-and DV-groups, see Table 3). These phenomena indicate that a heterolateral right-left fusion corresponds to a natural and hence harmonic connection, comparable with a normal embryo, where the left part of an anlage interacts with its right part during development. In contrast, a left-left or right-right connection is disharmonic, especially when viewed from the point of the field theory (see later). Thus, these connections provide only inadequate requirements for the developing of transindividual mirror symmetries of organ pairs.

In non-homopolar fused parabionts, a main symmetry plain is obtained by a rotation of one parabiont until a position is reached that is analog to a homopolar position (Fig. 2b–d). However, in this case the main symmetry plain is not identical with the plain of fusion. Dorsoventral polarity of the amphibian embryo is illustrated by the fact that dorsal-dorsal fusion results in a significantly enhanced organ pair symmetrisation, when compared to the ventral-ventral fusion type. It should be noted that the dorsal regions of the amphibian embryo (dorsal lip and roof of the blastopore as primary inducers, the neural tube as secondary inducer) have a crucial influence on the critical morphogenetic processes of blastema formation and generation of the organ anlagen during the gastrula, neurula, and postneurula stages. Earlier publications by Yamada (1940) and von Woellwarth (1957) suggest the same. The reason for the in part considerable differences between the organs of parabiotic twins with respect to their degree of symmetrisation within one experimental group (e.g. Ho-N and He-N, Tables 2 and 3) remains to be elucidated.

I would like to emphasise the point that the process of transindividual organ symmetrisation is not restricted to individuals of the same species, but is also effective with embryos of different species and even families such as *Triturus* (Salamandriae) and *Ambystoma* (Ambystomatidae). The underlying development process resulting in organ symmetrisation is apparently of a fundamental nature and not related to species-specific peculiarities.

It is remarkable that the phenomenon of transindividual organ symmetry in twins is hardly considered in recent publications. Levin et al. (1996) reported frequent heart inversions in the right embryo of chicken twin embryos, but gave no numbers about the frequency of a transindividual heart mirror symmetry with normal left situs. The same is true for twin embryos from *Xenopus*, which also exhibit frequent heart inversions in certain experiments, but where no quantitative data were reported about the frequency of transindividual heart mirror symmetry (Hyatt & Yost, 1998). Finally, the same is true for the paper from Nascone and Mercola (1997) concerning twin embryos from *Xenopus*. Again, transindividual heart mirror symmetries were obviously observed but not reported quantitatively.

The mirror symmetry, from which the bilateral symmetry as the dominant symmetry in the animal kingdom (Bilateria) is a special case, can be found in the animal kingdom in innumerable morphogenetic processes as a striking principle of development. This is illustrated by the following examples:

1. Symmetrisation of asymmetric fusion embryos (''Verbandskeime'') in amphibians (Mangold, 1920; Mangold & Seidel, 1927; Wang, 1933).
2. Regeneration of asymmetric fragments of the body to a complete harmonic and symmetric adult (individual) worm and symmetric heteromorphoses in Turbellaria (Kühn, 1965; Lus, 1926; Morgan, 1904).

3. Symmetric malformations, hypermorphoses, and regenerations of extremities, other appendages of the body and parts of the body (Bateson, 1894; Bohn, 1974a,b; Kolbow, 1928; Pfannestiel, 1984; Wilhelmi, 1923; Woitkewitsch, 1959; among others).

4. Imaginal disk experiments in insects (Kroeger, 1958, 1959a,b; Rahn, 1972).

5. Symmetries of pattern in butterfly wings (Kühn, 1965; Süffert, 1929).

6. Mirror symmetric duplications in Protozoa (Ciliata) (Frankel, 1991; Jerka-Dziadosz, 1983).

7. Formation of microskeletons in Holothuria (Echinodermata) (Wilhelmi, 1920).

To these and other conspicuous symmetries and symmetrisation in development can be added the frequent transindividual mirror images of parabiotic larvae, twins, or conjoined twins, as well as the conspicuous symmetry of the extremities in newt parabionts (see Fig. 5). (See later analysis of the appearance of symmetry in regard to the field concept.)

Right–left Axis and Dominance of Side

Today scientists, working on problems concerning the right–left organ symmetry, usually argue with a direct and causal correlation between the form and laterality of the heart and the gut, or of other morphological traits of the right–left axis. Just one example: Hyatt and Yost (1998) state that, after a certain experimental regimen, 75% of the hearts are inverted, from which 90% also exhibit gut inversions. They argue that "the entire left–right axis was inverted" (p. 39). Thus, the left–right axis is fixed here from the form and laterality of two inner organs. This kind of right–left determination has to be completely rejected for the following three reasons:

1. The principal reason that: "Once the first two axes are in place, so, by definition is the third, the left/right axis" (Hoyle, Brown & Wolpert, 1992, p. 1071). To be precise the term "definition" is not completely correct. This was discussed by Ludwig (1932), who wrote that only by *demonstration* can a side be quoted as left or right, while a definition of left and right is impossible.

2. From a morphological point of view, not only is the outer form symmetric, but the skeleton, muscle system, nerves, and large vessels, as well as the most inner organs (lung, kidney, brain, etc.) also have a distinct symmetric appearance (minor asymmetries, e.g. in lungs, can be neglected). Concerning the entire form of the vertebrate organism, it seems to me that some authors focus too much on the asymmetry of the heart and gut.

3. Because of the phenomenon of different normal laterality or inverse laterality in different organs (heterotaxis) it is completely impossible to deduce "right" or "left" from the form or laterality of one or more organs. In the example under discussion this would lead to a chaotic situation. Studying the form and laterality of single asymmetric organs, it is only possible to describe the relation of a single organ to the left–right axis that has already and independently been defined for the whole organism.

Heterotaxis, meaning the separation of asymmetric organs in respect to their situs, occurs frequently in my studies, especially in parabiotic pairs with high inversion numbers. Admittedly there is a vast concordance of the organ situs, especially in relatively less expressed organ inversions, but the high inversion numbers suggest that the anlagen of the individual organs (gut, heart, habenular nuclei, vitelline vein) comprise a certain independence, which becomes apparent during disturbances in development (von Kraft, 1969b). Comparable observations of heterotaxis have been made in *Xenopus* (Hyatt & Yost, 1998; Ryan et al., 1998; Sampath et al., 1997; Yost, 1992), mouse (Layton, 1976), and chick embryo (Levin et al., 1997).

What does side dominance mean? In the development of the vertebrate heart a variety of embryological observations and experiments have unequivocally shown a dominance of the left heart anlage, indicating a left dominance in the normal development of this organ (Bailly, 1963; Bride, 1974; Copenhaver, 1926; DeHaan, 1959; Ekman, 1925; Goerttler, 1928; Ichikawa, 1942; Zwirner & Kuhlo, 1964). The vitelline vein of the *Triturus* embryo develops as an initially symmetric and, in the anterior part of the body, bifurcated blood island, but later evolves into the main vessel of the intestinal vein system directed to the left and towards the heart (normal situs, see earlier and Fig. 9a) with a concomitant reduction of the right branch (Brauns, 1940; von Kraft, 1971b). In Ho-S parabiotic twins with two parallel, normally developed vitelline veins (Fig. 9b), there is almost invariably an obliteration of the vein directed to the right individual and accordingly a persistence of the left one (von Kraft, 1973). These and other observations are in agreement with results obtained in experimentally produced amphibian twins and duplicated larvae which always have a normal situs in the left, but frequently an inverse situs in the right partial organism. Based on these observations Ludwig (1932) postulated left-to-right and right-to-left gradients of agents ("L-Agens" and "R-Agens", respectively) in the embryo, with a usually more dominant L-agent. Related ideas can be found in contemporary theories using the term "morphogen" in a different meaning (e.g. Brown & Lander, 1993).

A first detailed discussion on this topic was produced by von Woellwarth (1950) (see also Oppenheimer, 1974). Further very extensive discussions can be found by Corballis and Morgan with comments of several authors (1978/1980). The latter authors published a very detailed "left-hand side hypothesis", suggesting a left-to-right gradient with dominance of the left-hand side. The dominance of the left-hand side discussed here may be interpreted as a morphogenetic dominance (von Kraft, 1971a) in view of the definitions given earlier (see Individual Situses of the Asymmetric Organs and "Unilateral Dominance") A different definition of unilateral dominance, i.e. physiologic inversion asymmetry (von Kraft, 1971a), is deduced from the possible induction of organ inversions by unilateral defects. Defects on the left-hand side of the embryo, but not those in the right-hand side, are thought to weaken the dominance of the gradient and cause organ inversions, based on the hypothesis of the "dominance of the left-hand side", e.g. Ludwig's postulation of gradients ("agent hypothesis"). In individual organisms, but not in duplicated organisms or artificially produced twins, such a definition predicts observations that are directly opposed to those summarised in Table 4. This definition interprets the stronger influence exerted by left-hand side defects as dominant due to increased lability or sensitivity of the embryo's left-hand side to external disturbances, and not as an increased resistance leading to undisturbed development of normal organ situs. This "physiologic" definition is mentioned here only because of its crucial role in the discussion of unilateral dominance.

Taken together, the results of the parabiotic experiments definitely contradict a special and generalising "'left hypothesis'", which has been discussed previously (von Kraft, 1982, 1986, 1995b). In addition, such direct contradictions have been revealed in some of my earlier studies on single animals (von Kraft, 1968b, 1970). Some data from the parabiotic experiments point to a change of side dominance during the development of the embryo (for example see numbers of experimental group Ho-G and Ho-N in Tables 2 and 4), and this is also true for certain experimental results from single animals (von Kraft, 1968a,b). Remarkably, a change of side dominance has been described during the development of the chicken heart (De Haan, 1959). It is difficult to achieve compatibility of a left dominance hypothesis with the relatively frequent occurrence of heterotaxis. The conception of regions or fields of the organ anlagen that are largely autonomous during certain developmental stages, are able to interact over a considerable distance (see parabiotic twins fused in a xenopolar manner, Fig. 11), and which produce an organ-specific pair situs, appears to be more appropriate for the interpretation of the experimental observations. In this context it should be noted that the three organs studied here stem from different germ layers: the intestinal tract stems from the entodermal layer, the heart and vitelline vein system stem from the mesodermal layer, and the nuclei habenulae of the diencephalon stem from the ectodermal layer.

Recent investigations have not added much new knowledge about the problem of side dominance. The reason is that they focus predominantly on the heart asymmetry, where left dominance has already been proven (see earlier). Transplantation experiments in chick embryos also confirm the left dominance of the heart anlage (Hoyle et al., 1992). The experiments of Smith et al. (1997) on chick heart anlagen can be interpreted in a similar way. In twins of chick embryos, the frequency of heart inversions differed, depending on the position of the conjoined twins (Levin et al., 1996). Studies on embryos of *Xenopus* also led to some different results. Injection of a variety of substances in different concentrations revealed much more frequent heart and gut inversions after a right side injection, compared to left-hand inversions (Sampath et al., 1997). According to my criteria of side dominance this can be interpreted as a left dominance. Similar results were obtained by Hyatt, Lohr, and Yost (1996) after injection of BVgl. This study also showed the complete dependence of the heart and gut inversion frequency on the kind of substance being injected (Hyatt et al., 1996). This has to be borne in mind when the inversion numbers obtained by Nascone and Mercola (1997) are interpreted: in heart development of artificially created conjoined twins the heart situs was mostly normal in left secondary twins, and always normal in left primary twins. In the case of a right secondary twin the heart situs was also mostly normal, but when Xwnt-8 was used, heart situs was normal in only 45%. In right primary twins the heart situs was mostly inverted. Taken together, these results indicate that one cannot speak of a left dominance. The further twin experiments from Hyatt and Yost (1998) have to be interpreted similarly. Again, only the heart development was analysed and the data obtained were strongly dependent on the position of the cells being injected and the kind of substance being used.

Remarkable asymmetries are revealed in more recent molecular biological studies in respect to the gene expression during different embryonic stages of the quoted experimental models (chick, mouse, *Xenopus*). Important genes influential for the laterality of organs, especially for the heart, were Shh (primary symmetrically expressed, changing to left-hand side expression beside Hensen's node), cNR-1 (expressed left-hand sided), and cAct-RIIa (expressed right-hand sided). These asymmetric expression patterns occurred during different embryonic stages and changed during embryonic development (Levin et al., 1995, 1996). As described by different authors, the Pitx2 gene was expressed strongly left-hand sided in all three experimental organisms (Logan et al., 1998; Piedra et al., 1998; Ryan et al., 1998; Yoshioka et al., 1998). The essential question of the ontogenetic relationship between the asymmetry of early gene expression and a subsequent organ asymmetry will not be discussed here.

Developmental Aspects of Organ Asymmetry

Most authors working in the field of emphibian developmental biology use embryos during the gastrula and neurula stage. In recent studies early pregastrula stages have been used more often in *Xenopus* (see later). Experimental studies of asymmetry on pregastrula stages of *Triturus* have been published by Mangold (1921, transient constriction without twin formation), Wehrmaker (1969, X-ray radiation and treatment with lithium), von Kraft (1969a, UV-radiation), and von Woellwarth (1970, induction of defects). In none of these studies was a higher incidence of organ inversion observed compared to controls. This indicates that, although in pregastrula stages the normal organ situs is genetically "preformed", the organ symmetry cannot be changed by external inflows (phase of predetermination). In contrast, the same methods applied to gastrula stages of the same species led to an increase of gut and heart inversions (von Kraft, 1968b; von Woellwarth, 1950; Wehrmaker, 1969). The same results were achieved with gastrula from *Ambystoma* (von Kraft, 1970). So determination of the organ asymmetry is onset in the gastrula stage and extends until the end of neurulation. Different experimental approaches, such as the parabiotic experiments, can change the organ situs markedly during neurulation, with a gradual decline during proceeding of this stage (phase of determination). Explanation experiments in *Xenopus* revealed a significant decrease of heart inversion when neurulation proceeded (Danos & Yost, 1996). This indicates that at the end of neurulation changes of the situs become impossible and the situs of the heart is irreversibly determined. Also in heart, the morphological shaping of the asymmetry occurs much later.

The irreversibly determined embryo at the tail-bud stage marks the beginning of a new developmental phase (post-determination phase) in which an invariable "virtual asymmetry" of the organs is present which has not yet become morphologically visible, as has been shown by Stark (Stark & von Kraft, 1993). The vitelline vein, as the main vessel of the intestinal venous system, constitutes an exception to a certain degree (see earlier, "Intestinal Venous System"). During consecutive developmental stages these "virtually" determined asymmetries become morphologically evident, first with heart and vitelline vein, then with the intestinal tract, and finally with the nuclei habenulae (Fig. 12). Then the embryo or the juvenile larva enters into the fourth and last developmental phase with respect to its organ asymmetry, which can be called the phase of beginning morphological lateral differentiation (phase of differentiation). The entire process of organ asymmetry development can thus be divided into four clearly distinguished phases (Fig. 12). Parabiotic experiments, applying an optimal way of fusion (Ho-, Xe-, and DD-fusion groups, Tables 2 and 5) were extremely useful for the induction of high numbers of organ inversions. For that reason these kinds of experiments were appropriate to study the end of the phase of determination. In all carefully analysed animals (chick, mouse, *Xenopus*) embryonic stages with asymmetric gene expression have been described, preceding by far the morphological asymmetry of the organs under investigation (mostly only the heart) Levin, 1997; Levin et al., 1995, 1997; Lowe et al., 1996; Pagán-Westphal & Tabin, 1998; Ryan et al., 1998; Wood, 1997). In *Xenopus*, asymmetric gene expression was described in the neurula stage (Lowe et al., 1996), but mostly in the postneurula stage (Hyatt et al., 1996; Hyatt & Yost, 1998; Lowe et al., 1996; Nascone & Mercola, 1997; Sampath et al., 1997), which is comparable to the postdetermination phase in *Triturus*. The correlation of asymmetric gene expression and organ situs is close

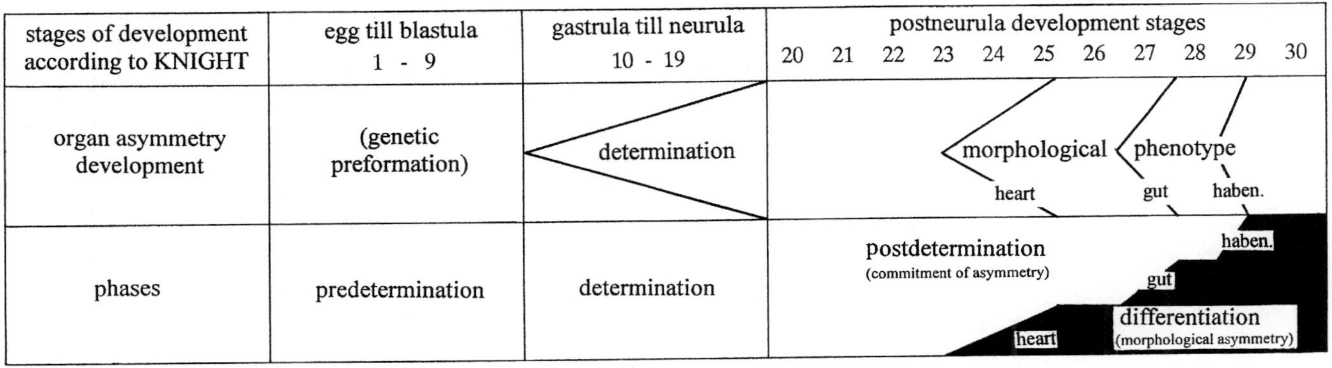

stages of development according to KNIGHT	egg till blastula 1 - 9	gastrula till neurula 10 - 19	postneurula development stages 20 21 22 23 24 25 26 27 28 29 30
organ asymmetry development	(genetic preformation)	determination	morphological phenotype — heart, gut, haben.
phases	predetermination	determination	postdetermination (commitment of asymmetry) — differentiation (morphological asymmetry) — heart, gut, haben.

FIG. 12. Developmental phases of intestinal tract, heart, and nuclei habenulae with respect to their stage of determination and the morphologic realisation of their asymmetry. See text for more details.

in some studies (e.g. Pagán-Westphal & Tabin, 1998), but less close in others (e.g. Hyatt & Yost, 1998; Piedra et al., 1998).

While manipulations of pregastrula stage in *Triturus* hardly ever led to organ inversions (phase of predetermination), other experimental approaches in early embryonic stages (cleavage stage) of *Xenopus* revealed a high number of organ inversions, mostly investigated in the heart. In these experiments specific substances were microinjected in single blastomeres, which sometimes induced the development of conjoined twins (Danos & Yost, 1995; Hyatt et al., 1996; Hyatt & Yost, 1998; Nascone & Mercola, 1997; Sampath et al., 1997). A direct comparison of these data with those obtained from the experiments with *Triturus* seems difficult because of the different experimental approaches.

Genes and Morphogenetic Field

Beside the results concerning the laterality of the inner organs in parabiotic twins, the transindividual and dominant mirror symmetry is of special interest, suggesting a comprehensive process of symmetrisation (von Kraft, 1976b; see also Fig. 10). Certainly, a complete inversion of the situs (situs inversus) is basically a comprehensive process combining a variety of different organs. From this fact it seems possible to envision the term "morphogenetic field", which was originally introduced by Alexander Gurwitsch (1922, 1927, 1930) and Paul Weiss (1925, 1926) as a theoretical concept alternative to the more reductionistic and cellular concept of development. The spirit of the concept of the morphogenetic field was characterised by Hans Driesch, quoted in Gurwitsch (1922, p. 383): "*Das Schicksal eines Teiles wird durch seine Lage zum Ganzen bestimmt*" (The fate of a part is determined by its position relative to the whole). Recently, Rupert Sheldrake has reintroduced the term morphogenetic field in a remarkable way (Sheldrake, 1981).

Linked to the sentence from Driesch just quoted, Gurwitsch (1922, p. 383) wrote: "*Das 'Ganze' tritt uns damit als ein realer Entwicklungsfaktor entgegen*" (The 'whole' advances towards us as a real factor of development), and Alfred Kühn (1943, p. 376) said of basically different developmental processes: "*Die Form wird durch einen überzelligen Vorgang geprägt*" (Form is determined by a supracellular process). A similar statement came from Bernhard Dürken (1929, p. 152): "*Das Feld ist der Ort des embryonalen Geschehens und der Formbildung*' (The morphogenetic field is the scene of the developmental events and the establishment of the form). Proven by numerous experimental studies, the dimension of time is an essential and basic property of the morphogenetic field. This means that the morphogenetic field is successively subdivided into partial fields in a regular and dynamic manner (Gurwitsch, 1927, 1930; Vogt, 1923; Weiss, 1925). This process of the evolution of the field, sometimes also designated as "field decay", was circumscribed by Saunders (1968, p. 65) as follows: "As development proceeds, reactions within the comprehensive fields leads to the establishment of smaller fields of increasing specialisation, i.e. concerned with only limited patterns of differentiation.'' It is not possible here to quote more important aspects and partially controversially discussed properties of the ''field''. The same is true for the innumerable experimental data of classical developmental biology since Roux, Driesch, and Spemann (1936), which led with a sort of inner logic to the idea of the morphogenetic field (see also Bautzmann, 1955; French, Bryant, & Bryant, 1976; Gerisch, 1971; Hadorm, Bertani, & Gallera, 1949; Krause, 1962; Kühn, 1965; Vogt, 1923). Very important data about the morphogenetic field were obtained from regeneration experiments (Goss, 1969). In particular, the experimental studies from Kroeger (1958, 1959, 1960) on insects pointed to symmetry properties in respect of the field phenomenon.

Already in 1922 Gurwitsch spoke of an ''overestimation of the term 'cell' '' as used by many biologists, and in 1925 Weiss was aware of an ''overestimation of single cell events''. Such an overestimation still exists among contemporary cell and molecular biologists, especially in respect to the theoretical evaluation and interpretation of their experimental data, which *per se* are important research results. The reductionistic approach, rooted in the time of Gurwitsch, Spemann, and Weiss, has already reached the scale of subcellular structures and molecules. The aim is to understand and explain in molecular terms more complex morphological forms, like the special problems of laterality on a macro-morphological scale. This becomes particularly evident in the model from Brown and Wolpert (1990), which almost all scientists working in the field of laterality, have obviously accepted. . Three major aspects of this model are:

1. The assumption of an asymmetry of molecules (''molecular handedness'').
2. The term ''chance'' (''mechanism for random generation of asymmetry''). (This term is useless for the interpretation of the results from parabiotic experiments and should be substituted by the concept of differently strong antagonistic forces, leading to normal, partly invers, or total invers organ situs.)
3. The use of the problematic term ''interpretation'' (''tissue specific interpretation process'', Brown & Wolpert, 1990, p. 1).

As far as I know the most striking critique of the cellular and molecular biological reductionism came from Paul Weiss. In accordance with the original concept of the morphogenetic field he postulated a ''Hierarchy of Wholes and Parts''. In this concept every scale has its own rules or degrees of freedom, which are subordinated under a superordinated whole. Weiss (1969, p. 395) summarised this as follows: ''Hierarchic stepwise delegation of tasks to sub-systems is ostensibly nature's efficient device to let an organism keep order without having to deal with its trillions of molecules directly.'' More remarkable is the critique of Weiss of such ''pretentious anthropomorphic terms'' like ''dictate'', ''inform'', ''interpret'', ''response'', ''control'', ''read'', ''initiate'', "execute", "signalling molecules" etc., obviously "borrowed from the vocabulary of human system behaviour, especially the brain" and applied to cell structures and molecules, a "logical flaw", as Weiss (1969) properly remarks.

Finally, most scientists admit that, in spite of remarkable progress in our knowledge about innumerable molecular and subcellular details, we do not understand how macromolecular processes and the form of organs are realised by genes or effects of genes. In parallel, speculations about this and about possible processes on the lowest molecular and structural scales are dominating. From these circumstances, a warning from Paul Weiss (1953, p. 210) can be understood:

> ... the illusion, that the mere identification of physico-chemical systems can have much explanatory value unless their formal order of operation in the living system has likewise been revealed. It is of greater pragmatic value to set forth at least formal models of phenomena known to occur in living systems than to ignore or even deny the occurrence of those phenomena just because our present incomplete, oversimplified, and elementary schemes cannot account for them. Field phenomena in supercellular systems are a firm reality to all those observers and analysts of living phenomena who have not deliberately confined themselves to the investigation of elementary and fragmentary processes in which field properties can be legitimately ignored.

REFERENCES

Bailly, S. (1963). Organogenèse du coeur et des arcs aortiques chez les Triton *Pleurodeles waltlii* Michah. après fissuration de l'ébauche cardiaque embryonnaire. *Bull. biol. France Belg, 97*, 627–642.

Bateson, W. (1894). *Materials for the study of variation.* London, New York: Macmillan & Co.

Bautzmann, H. (1955). Die Problemlage des Spemannschen Organisators. *Die Naturwissenschaften, 42*, 286–294.

Bergquist, H. (1932). Zur Morphologie des Zwischenhirns bei niederen Wirbeltieren. *Acta Zoologica, 13*, 57–303.

Bohn, H. (1974a,b). Extent and properties of the regeneration field in the larval legs of cockroaches (*Leucophaea maderae*). II. Conformation by transplantation experiments. *J. Embryol. exp. Morph., 32*, 1, 69–79. III. Origin of the tissues and determination of symmetry properties in the regenerates. *J. Embryol. exp. Morph., 32*(1), 81–98.

Brauns, A. (1940). Untersuchungen zur Ermittlung der Entstehung der roten Blutzellen in der Embryonalentwicklung der Urodelen. *Roux' Archiv der Entwicklungsmechanik der Organismen, 140*, 741–789.

Bride, M. (1974). Autodifférenciation du mésoderme précardiaque d'Amphibians Anoures en culture in vitro. *C.R. Acad. Sc. Paris, 278*, 777–780.

Brown, N.A., & Lander, A. (1993). On the other hand... *Nature, 363*, 303–304.

Brown, N.A., & Wolpert, L. (1990). The development of handedness in left/right asymmetry. *Development, 109*, 1–9.

Copenhaver, W.M. (1926). Experiments on the development of the heart of *Amblystoma punctatum*. *J. Exp. Zool., 43*, 321–371.

Corballis, M.C., & Morgan, M.J. (and commentators) (1978/1980). On the biological basis of human laterality: I. Evidence for a maturational left–right gradient. II. The mechanisms of inheritance. *Behavioral and Brain Science, 2,* 261–336, and *3,* 476–482.

Danos, M.C., & Yost, H.J. (1995). Linkage of cardiac left–right asymmetry and dorsal-anterior development in *Xenopus. Development, 121,* 1467–1474.

Danos, M.C., & Yost, H.J. (1996). Role of notochord in specification of cardiac left–right orientation in zebrafish and *Xenopus. Devel. Biol., 177,* 96–103.

De Haan, R.L. (1959). Cardia bifida and the development of pacemaker functin in the early chick heart. *Develop. Biol., 1,* 586–602.

Dürken, B. (1929). *Grundtiß der Entwicklungsmechanik.* Berlin: Bornträger.

Ekman, G. (1925). Experimentelle Beiträge zur Herzentwicklung der Amphibien. *Roux' Archiv der Entwicklungsmechanik der Organismen, 106,* 320–352.

Fankhauser, G. (1930). Die Entwicklungspotenzen diploidkerniger Hälften des ungefurchten Tritoneies. *Roux' Archiv der Entwicklungsmechanik der Organismen, 122,* 671–735.

Frankel, J. (1991). Intracellular handedness in ciliates. In *Biological asymmetry and handedness* (pp. 73–93). Chichester, UK: John Wiley & Sons.

French, V., Bryant, P.J., & Bryant, S.V. (1976). Pattern regulation in epimorphic fields. *Science, 193,* 969–981.

Gerisch, G. (1971). Periodische Signale steuern die Musterbildung in Zellverbänden. *Naturwiss, 58,* 430–438.

Goerttler K. (1928). Die Bedeutung der ventrolateralen Mesodermbezirke für die Herzanlage der Amphibienkeime. *Verhandlungen der Anatomischen Gesellschaft 1928, Anatomischer Anzeiger, Supplement, 66,* 132–139.

Goss, R.J. (1969). *Principles of regeneration.* New York: Academic Press.

Gurwitsch, A. (1922). Über den Begriff des Embryonalen Feldes. *Roux' Archiv der Entwicklungsmechanik der Organismen, 51,* 383–415.

Gurwitsch, A. (1927). Weiterbildung und Verallgemeinerung des Feldbegriffes. *Roux' Archiv der Entwicklungsmechanik der Organismen, 112,* 433–454.

Gurwitsch, A. (1930). Die histologischen Grundlagen der Biologie. (4. Teil: *Theorie des Feldes,* pp. 229–306). Jena: Gustav Fischer.

Hadorn, E., Bertani, G., & Gallera, J. (1949). Regulationsfähigkeit und Feldorganisation der männlichen Genitalimaginalscheibe von *Drosophila melanogaster. Roux' Archiv der Entwicklungsmechanik der Organismen, 144,* 31–70.

Hoyle, C., Brown, N.A., & Wolpert, L. (1992). Development of left/right handedness in the chick heart. *Development, 115,* 1071–1078.

Hyatt, B.A., Lohr, J.L., & Yost, H.J. (1996). Initiation of vertebrate left–right axis formation by maternal Vg1. *Nature, 384,* 62–65.

Hyatt, B.A., & Yost, H.J. (1998). The left–right coordinator: The role of Vg1 in organizing left–right axis formation. *Cell, 93,* 37–46.

Ichikawa, M. (1942). Studies on the double monsters in the newt, *Triturus pyrrhogaster,* with special reference to the origin of their development. *Mem. College Sci. Kyoto, Imper. Univ. SerB, 17,* 2, 2, 175–226.

Jerka-Dziadosz, M. (1983). The origin of mirror-image symmetry doublet cells in the hypotrich ciliate *Paraurostyla weissei. Roux' Arch Dev Biol, 192,* 179–188.

Kolbow, H. (1928). Experimentell verursachte Bildung von Armen aus ursprünglichem Beinmaterial bei Triton. *Roux' Archiv der Entwicklungsmechanik der Organismen, 113,* 12–38.

Krause, G. (1962). Die Entwicklungsphysiologie kreuzweise verdoppelter Embryonen. *Embryologia, 6 (Mangold Festschrift Suppl.),* 355–386.

Kreht, H. (1939). Form und Zellaufbau des Ganglion habenulae und der Area subhabenularis bei Anuren, Urodelen und Gymnophionen. *Zeitschrift mikroskopisch-anatomischer Forschung, 46,* 470–487.

Kroeger, H. (1958). Über Doppelbildungen in die Leibeshöhle verpflanzter Flügelimaginalscheiben von *Ephestia kühniella Z. Roux' Archiv der Entwicklungsmechanik der Organismen, 150,* 401–424.

Kroeger, H. (1959a). Determinationsmosaike aus kombiniert implantierten Imaginalscheiben von *Ephestia kühniella* Zeller. *Roux' Archiv der Entwicklungsmechanik der Organismen, 151*, 113–135.

Kroeger, H. (1959b). The genetic control of genital morphology in *Drosophila*. *Roux' Archiv der Entwicklungsmechanik der Organismen, 151*, 301–322.

Kroeger, H. (1960). Die Entstehung von Form im morphogenetischen Feld. *Naturwissenschaften, 47*, 148–159.

Kühn, A. (1943). Die Ausprägung organischer Formen in verschiedenen Dimensionen und die Grundfragen der Entwicklungsphysiologie. *Naturwissenschaften, 31*, 373–383.

Kühn, A. (1965). *Vorlesungen über Entwicklungsphysiologie*. Berlin, Heidelberg, New York: Springer-Verlag.

Kühn, A. (1971). *Lectures on developmental physiology*. Berlin: Springer-Verlag.

Layton, W.M. (1976). Random determination of a developmental process. *J. Heredity, 67*, 336–338.

Levin, M. (1997). Left–right asymmetry in vertebrate embryogenesis. *BioEssays, 19*(4), 287–296.

Levin, M., Johnson, R.L., Stern, C.D., Kuehn, M., & Tabin, C. (1995). A molecular pathway determining left–right asymmetry in chick embryogenesis. *Cell, 82*, 803–814.

Levin, M., Pagan, S., Roberts, D., Cooke, J., Kuehn, M.R., & Tabin, C. (1997). Left/right patterning signals and the independent regulation of different aspects of *Situs* in the chick embryo. *Devel. Biol., 189*, 57–67.

Levin, M., Roberts, D., Holmes, L.B., & Tabin, C. (1996). Laterality defects in conjoined twins. *Nature, 384*, 321.

Logan, M., Pagán-Westphal, S.M., Smith, D.M., Paganessi, L., & Tabin, C.J. (1998). The transcription factor Pitx2 mediates situs-specific morphogenesis in response to left–right asymmetric signals. *Cell, 94*, 307–317.

Lowe, L.A., Supp, D.M., Sampath, K., Yokoyama, T., Wright, C.V.E., Potter, S.S., Overbeek, P., & Kuehn, M.R. (1996). Conserved left–right asymmetry of nodal expression and alterations in murine *situs inversus*. *Nature, 381*, 158–161.

Ludwig, W. (1932, reprinted 1970). *Das Rechts–Links-Problem im Tierreich und beim Menschen*. Berlin, Heidelberg, New York: Springer-Verlag.

Lus, J. (1926). Regenerationsversuche an marinen Tricladen. *Roux' Archiv der Entwicklungsmechanik der Organismen, 108*, 203–227.

Mangold, O. (1920). Fragen der Regulation und Determination an umgeordneten Furchungsstadien und verschmolzenen Keimen von Triton. *Roux' Archiv der Entwicklungsmechanik der Organismen, 47*, 249–301.

Mangold, O. (1921). Situs inversus bei Triton. *Roux' Archiv der Entwicklungsmechanik der Organismen, 48*, 505–516.

Mangold, O., & Seidel, F. (1927). Homoplastiche und heteroplastische Verschmelzung ganzer Tritonkeime. *Roux' Archiv der Entwicklungsmechanik der Organismen, 111*, 593–665.

Morgan, M.J. (1991). The asymmetrical genetic determination of laterality: flatfish, frogs and human handedness. In G.R. Bock & J. Marsh (Eds.), *Biological Asymmetry and Handedness* (pp.234–250), *Ciba Foundation Symposium 162*. Chichester, UK: John Wiley & Sons.

Morgan, T.H. (1904). Regeneration of heteromorphic tails in posterior pieces of *Planaria simplicissima*. *J. Exp. Zool., 1*, 385–393.

Nascone, N., & Mercola, M. (1997). Organizer induction determines left–right asymmetry in *Xenopus*. *Devel. Biol., 189*, 68–78.

Oppenheimer, J.M. (1974). Asymmetry revisited. *Amer. Zool., 14*, 867–879.

Pagán-Westphal, S.M., & Tabin, C.J. (1998). The transfer of left–right positional information during chick embryogenesis. *Cell, 93*, 25–35.

Pfannenstiel, H.-D. (1984). The ventral nerve cord signals positional information during segment formation in an annelid (*Ophryotrocha puerilis*, Polychaeta). *Roux's Arch Dev Biol, 194*, 32–36.

Piedra, M.E., Icardo, J.M., Albajar, M., Rodriguez-Rey, J.C., & Ros, M.A. (1998). Pitx2 participates in the late phase of the pathway controlling left–right asymmetry. *Cell*, *94*, 319–324.

Przibram, H. (1907). Equilibrium of animal form. *J. Exper. Zool.*, *5*, 259–284.

Przibram, H. (1921). Die Bruch-Dreifachbildung im Tierreiche. *Roux' Archiv der Entwicklungsmechanik der Organismen*, *48*, 205–444.

Rahn, P. (1972). Untersuchungen zur Entwicklung von Ganz-und Teilimplantaten der Flügelimaginalscheibe von *Ephestia kühniella Z. Roux' Archiv der Entwicklungsmechanik der Organismen*, *170*, 48–82.

Ruud, G., & Spemann, H. (1922). Die Entwicklung isolierter dorsaler und lateraler Gastrulahälften von *Triton taeniatus* und *alpestris*, ihre Regulation und Postgeneration. *Roux' Archiv der Entwicklungsmechanik der Organismen*, *52*, 95–166.

Ryan, A.K., Blumberg, B., Rodriguez-Esteban, C., Yonei-Tamura, S., Tamura, K., Tsukui, T., de la Peña, J., Sabbagh, W., Greenwald, J., Choe, S., Norris, D.P., Robertson, E.J., Evans, R.M., Rosenfeld, M.G., & Belmonte, J.C.I. (1998). Pitx2 determines left–right asymmetry of internal organs in vertebrates. *Nature*, *394*, 545–551.

Sampath, K., Cheng, A.M.S., Frisch, A., & Wright, C.V.E. (1997). Functional differences among *Xenopus nodal-related* genes in left–right axes determination. *Development*, *124*, 3293–3302.

Saunders, J.W. Jr. (1968). *Animal morphogenesis*. New York: The Macmillan Company.

Sheldrake, R. (1981). *A new science of life*. London: Blond & Briggs Ltd.

Smith, S.M., Dickman, E.D., Thompson, R.P., Sinning, A.R., Wunsch, A.M., & Markwald, R.R. (1997). Retinoic acid directs cardiac laterality and the expression of early markers of precardiac asymmetry. *Dev. Biol.*, *182*, 162–171.

Spemann, H. (1936). Experimentelle Beiträge zu einer Theorie der Entwicklung. Berlin: J. Springer. [*Embryonic Development and Induction.* Philadelphia: Garland Publ., 1988, USA.]

Spemann, H., & Falkenberg, H. (1919). Über asymmetrische Entwicklung und Situs inversus viscerum bei Zwillingen und Doppelbildungen. *Roux' Archiv der Entwicklungsmechanik der Organismen*, *45*, 371–422.

Stark, S., & von Kraft, A. (1993). Die Entwicklung der Asymmetrie von Darmtrakt, Herz und Nuclei habenulae des Zwischenhirns beim Bergmolch (*Triturus alpestris*). *Zoologische Jahrbücher, Abteilung für Anatomie und Ontogenie der Tiere*, *123*, 103–123.

Süffert, F. (1929). Morphologische Erscheinungsgruppen in der Flügelzeichnung der Schmetterlinge, insbesondere die Querbindenzeichnung. *Roux' Archiv der Entwicklungsmechanik der Organismen*, *120*, 299–383.

Vogt, W. (1923). Morphologische und physiologische Fragen der Primitiventwicklung, Versuche zu ihrer Lösung mittels vitaler Farbmarkierung. *Sitzungsber. d. Ges. Morph. Physiol. München*, *35*, 22–32.

von Kraft, A. (1968a). Larvengestalt und Eingeweide-Situs beim Alpenmolch (*Triturus alpestris*) nach halbseitiger UV-Bestrahlung von Neurula-und Nachneurula-Keimen. *Roux' Archiv der Entwicklungsmechanik der Organismen*, *160*, 259–297.

von Kraft, A. (1968b). Situs inversus beim Alpenmolch (*Triturus alpestris*) nach UV-Bestrahlung von Gastrula-Keimen. *Roux' Archiv der Entwicklungsmechanik der Organismen*, *161*, 351–374.

von Kraft, A. (1969a). Der Eingeweidesitus beim Alpenmolch *Triturus alpestris*) nach UV-Bestrahlung von Prägastrula-Stadien. *Roux' Archiv der Entwicklungsmechanik der Organismen*, *163*, 178–183.

von Kraft, A. (1969b). Die Situskorrelationen von Darmtrakt, Herz und Habenulakernen beim Alpenmolch (*Triturus alpestris*) nach UV-Bestrahlung in verschiedenen Entwicklungsstadien. *Zoologische Jahrbücher, Abteilung für Anatomie und Ontogenie der Tiere*, *86*, 615–633.

von Kraft, A. (1970). Veränderungen des Eingeweidesitus beim Axolotl (*Ambystoma mexicanum*) nach UV-Bestrahlung von Gastrula-und Neurulakeimen. *Zoologische Jahrbücher, Abteilung für Anatomie und Ontogenie der Tiere*, *87*, 224–240.

von Kraft, A. (1971a). Entstehung der Eingewide-Asymmetrie bei den Wirbeltieren. *Naturwissenschaftliche Rundschau, 24*, 142–151.

von Kraft, A. (1971b). Erscheinungsbild und Entwicklung der Darmdottervene und ihre Beziehung zur Eingeweide-Asymmetrie bei Urodelen. *W. Roux' Archiv der Entwicklungsmechanik der Organismen, 168*, 332–349.

von Kraft, A. (1973). Eingeweidesitus und Darmvenensystem bei parabiotischen, im Schwanzknospenstadium verschmolzenen Larven des Bergmolches (*Triturus alpestris*). *Zoologische Jahrbücher, Abteilung für Anatomie und Ontogenie der Tiere, 90*, 526–549.

von Kraft, A. (1976a). Symmetrie und Asymmetrie in der Morphogenese parabiotischer, im Neurulastadium verschmolzener Bergmolchlarven (*Triturus alpestris*). I. Äußere Gestalt und Extremitäten. *Zoologische Jahrbücher, Abteilung für Anatomie und Ontogenie der Tiere, 96*, 238–268.

von Kraft, A. (1976b). Symmetrie und Asymmetrie in der Morphogenese parabiotischer, im Neurulastadium verschmolzener Bergmolchlarven (*Triturus alpestris*). II. Innere Organe (Eingeweide, Habenulakerne, Darmvenensystem). *Zoologische Jahrbücher, Abteilung für Anatomie und Ontogenie der Tiere, 96*, 303–357.

von Kraft, A. (1980). Situs inversus der Eingeweide und Nuclei habenulae bei heteropolar verwachsenen Parabiose-Larven des Bergmolches (*Triturus alpestris*). *Zoologische Jahrbücher, Abteilung für Anatomie und Ontogenie der Tiere, 103*, 510–536.

von Kraft, A. (1981). Organasymmetrien bei stark altersverschiedenen, homopolar verwachsenen Parabiose-Larven des Bergmolches (*Triturus alpestris*). *Zoologische Jahrbücher, Abteilung für Anatomie und Ontogenie der Tiere, 106*, 87–103.

von Kraft, A. (1982). Die Beeinflußbarkeit der Organasymmetrie beim Bergmolch (*Triturus alpestris*) durch laterale Verwachsung alter ''Vorderteil-Neurulae'' mit jungen Neurulae (Anterior-Lateral-Parabionten). *Zoologische Jahrbücher, Abteilung für Anatomie und Ontogenie der Tiere, 107*, 71–84.

von Kraft, A. (1985). Spiegelsymmetrische Organbildung bei xenoplastischen Molch-Parabionten (Triturus-Ambystoma-Parabionten). *Verhandlungen der Anatomischen Gesellschaft, 79*, 583–585.

von Kraft, A. (1986). Situs inversus und Spiegelsymmetrie in der Organogenese von ''xenopolar'' im Neurulastadium verwachsenen Bergmolch-Parabionten (*Triturus alpestris*). *Zoologische Jahrbücher, Abteilung für Anatomie und Ontogenie der Tiere, 114*, 43–68.

von Kraft, A. (1990). Symmetrieverhältnisse und Dynamik des Darmvenensystems bei ''xenopolar'' im Neurula-Stadium verwachsenen Bergmolch-Parabionten (*Triturus alpestris*). *Zoologische Jahrbücher, Abteilung für Anatomie und Ontogenie der Tiere, 120*, 93–108.

von Kraft, A. (1991). Organsitus und Darmvenenverlauf bei im Neurulastadium dorso-ventral-polar verwachsenen Parabioselarven des Bergmolches (*Triturus alpestris*). *Zoologische Jahrbücher, Abteilung für Anatomie und Ontogenie der Tiere, 121*, 15–37.

von Kraft, A. (1995a). Die Symmetrieverhältnisse der Eingeweide, der Habenulakerne und des Darmvenensystems bei dorsal-dorsal und ventral-ventral verwachsenen Parabioselarven des Bergmolches (*Triturus alpestris*). *Ann. Anat., 177*, 61–72.

von Kraft. A. (1995b). Spiegelsymmetrische und ''linksdominante'' Organogenese bei im Gastrulastadium verschmolzenen Parabioselarven des Bergmolches (*Triturus alpestris*). *Ann. Anat., 177*, 367–374.

von Woellwarth, C. (1950). Experimentelle Untersuchungen über den Situs inversus der Eingeweide und der Habenula des Zwischenhirns bei Amphibien. *Roux' Archiv der Entwicklungsmechanik der Organismen, 144*, 178–256.

von Woellwarth, C. (1957). Zur Frage der Induktionsfelder in jungen Embryonalstadien der Amphibien. *Verhandlungen der Deutschen Zoologischen Gesellschaft, 1957 (Graz), Zoologischer Anzeiger, Supplement, 21*, 424–430.

von Woellwarth, C. (1970). Der Eingeweidesitus beim Alpenmolch (*Triturus alpestris*) nach

Materialdefekten im Ektoderm der Blastula. *W. Roux' Archiv der Entwicklungsmechanik der Organismen, 165*, 87–90.

Wang, S.C. (1933). Die regulative Entwicklung dorsal-lateraler Verbandskeime von *Triton taeniatus. Roux' Archiv der Entwicklungsmechanik der Organismen, 130*, 243–265.

Wehrmaker, A. (1969). Right–left asymmetry and situs inversus in *Triturus alpestris. Roux' Archiv der Entwicklungsmechanik der Organismen, 163*, 1–32.

Weiss, P. (1925). Unabhängigkeit der Extremitätenregeneration vom Skelett (bei *Triton cristatus*). *Roux' Archiv der Entwicklungsmechanik der Organismen, 104*, 359–394.

Weiss, P. (1926). Ganzregenerate aus halbem Extremitätenquerschnitt. *Roux' Archiv der Entwicklungsmechanik der Organismen, 107*, 1–53.

Weiss, P. (1953). Some introductory remarks on the cellular basis of differentiation. *J. Embryol. ex. Morph., 1*(3), 181–211.

Weiss, P. (1969). The living system: Determinism stratified. *Studium Generale, 22*, 361–400.

Wilhelmi, H. (1920). Ein Beitrag zur Theorie der organischen Symmetrie, der sich gründet auf die Analyse der Entwicklungskorrelationen bei der Skelettbildung der fußlosen Holothurien. *Roux' Archiv der Entwicklungsmechanik der Organismen, 46*, 210–258.

Wilhelmi, H. (1923). Über Transplantationen von Extremitätenanlagen mit Rücksicht auf das Symmetrieproblem. *Roux' Archiv der Entwicklungsmechanik der Organismen, 52*, 182–222.

Woitkewitsch, A.A. (1959). *Natürliche Mehrfachbildungen an Froschextremitäten.* Jena: Gustav Fischer.

Wood, W.B. (1997). Left–right asymmetry in animal development. *Annu. Rev. Cell Dev. Biol., 13*, 53–82.

Yamada, T. (1940). Beeinflussung der Differenzierungsleistung des isolierten Mesoderms von Molchkeimen durch zugefügtes Chorda-und Neuralmaterial. *Folia Anat. Jap., 19*, 131–197.

Yoshioka, H., Meno, C., Koshiba, K., Sugihara, M., Itoh, H., Ishimaru, Y., Inoue, T., Ohuchi, H, Semina, E.V., Murray, J.C., Hamada, H., & Noji, S. (1998). Pitx2, a bicoid-type homeobox gene, is involved in a left-signalling pathway in determination of left–right asymmetry. *Cell, 94*, 299–305.

Yost, H.J. (1991). Development of left–right axis in amphibians (pp.165–181). *Biological asymmetry and handedness. Ciba Foundation Symposium 162.* Chichester, UK: John Wiley & Sons.

Yost, H.J. (1992). Regulation of vertebrate left–right asymmetries by extracellular matrix. *Nature, 357*, 158–161.

Yost, H.J. (1995). Vertebrate left–right development. *Cell, 82*, 689–692.

Zwirner, R., & Kuhlo, B. (1964). Die prospektive Potenz der rechten und der linken Herzanlage (Ein experimenteller Beitrag zur Asymmetrie des Herzens). *Roux' Archiv der Entwicklungsmechanik der Organismen, 155*, 511–524.

LATERALITY, 1999, 4 (3), 257–264

Handedness in the NAS/NRC Twin Study

D.C. Ross, J. Jaffe, R.L. Collins, W. Page, & D. Robinette

New York State Psychiatric Institute, USA

In 1985, a hand preference survey was completed by 973 dizygotic and 1158 monozygotic male twin pairs, all veterans of World War II. This is the largest single twin study of handedness on record. As in state-of-the-art animal research, the laterality criterion was sensitive to both direction and consistency (degree, strong or weak) of handedness. Significant pairwise concordance was shown for the total group, and for consistency and directional factors separately. However, no zygosity differences were demonstrated.

INTRODUCTION

McManus (1980) reviewed 19 studies of hand preference in twins. Of these, 18 included both monozygotic (MZ) and dizygotic (DZ) twins; one had only MZ twins. Total sample sizes varied from 18 to 847. McManus concluded that the incidence of left handedness is the same in MZ and DZ twins and that the proportion of L–L, R–L, and R–R pairs in MZ twins cannot be generated from independent binomial distributions. The author noted that this failure to observe greater concordance in MZ than in DZ twins represents the "Achilles heel" of handedness genetics.

Concurrently, it was demonstrated that mice could be bred for consistency but not direction of "pawedness" (Collins, 1977, 1991). This helped to refocus the methodology of human assessment, leading to more sophisticated measures that took both factors into account.

Requests for reprints should be sent to D.C. Ross, Unit 19, New York State Psychiatric Institute, 722 West 168th Street, New York, NY 10032, USA.

Project: National Academy of Science/National Reserch Council Twin Study of Laterality as a Marker for Survival Fitness. J. Jaffe, P.I. From the Department of Psychiatry, Columbia University and the New York State Psychiatric Institute: Ross, D.C., NYSPI; Jaffe, J., NYSPI; Collins, R.L., Jackson Lab; Page, W., and Robinette, D. (deceased), Medical Follow-up Agency, NAS. Partially supported by Clinical Research Center Grant MH30906 and by a gift from Lore Kann.

The opinions and asserts contained herein are those of the authors and are not to be construed as reflecting the views or position of the National Academy of Sciences, the Institute of Medicine, or the National Reserch Council.

METHOD

The NAS/NRC Twin Registry consists of 15,924 male twin pairs, all veterans of World War II who have been followed for over 40 years. A re-survey in 1985 included questions dealing with putative markers for cerebral laterality genes. Our sample consists of 2131 twin pairs in which both twins were living when the data tape was created, 973 DZ and 1158 MZ, all of whom completed the laterality questionnaire. This provides a considerably larger number of twin pairs whose hand preference has been evaluated by the same criterion in one study than has been previously available.

In contrast to all prior MZ vs. DZ twin studies of handedness, we employed a laterality criterion that was sensitive to both direction and consistency of hand preference on five tasks (write, draw, throw, scissors, toothbrush), each of which was rated on a 5-point scale as 1 = always left, 2 = usually left, 3 = no preference, 4 = usually right, 5 = always right. This procedure was recommended by Bryden (1982) on the basis of a factor analysis of a much larger questionnaire. His composite score ranges from –1.0 to +1.0 in steps of 0.1. For the initial concordance analyses, this continuous measure was collapsed into five categories: –1.0 is Strong Left, –.9 to –.5 is Weak Left, –.4 to +.4 is Ambidextrous, +.5 to +.9 is Weak Right, and +1.0 is Strong Right.

In addition to the simple chi-square analyses described later, the data on consistency of handedness and direction of handedness were also analysed using a structural equations model. This approach makes use of polychoric and tetrachoric correlations (Kendler et al., 1992) that are calculated on the assumption that there are underlying, continuous distributions of liability to consistency and direction of handedness, respectively. The correlations are then used in a modelling process that estimates the size of latent variables that represent genetic, common environment, and unique environment factors. The fact that the MZ twins have twice the correlation for genes as DZ twins (i.e. 1.0 vs. .5) is built into these models (Neale & Cardon, 1992).

RESULTS

Directionality × Consistency Analyses

The number of twin pairs falling into each possible set of bivariate handedness categories is presented in Tables 1a and 1b, for DZ and MZ pairs, respectively. The distributions of twin pairs over the various categories does not appear very different for MZ and DZ twins. The two tables can be regarded as the result of a multinomial sampling with $5 \times 6 = 30$ categories, with the null hypothesis being that the probabilities for the 15 catgegories in the MZ table are the same as for the corresponding 15 categories in the DZ table. Thinking of the data, then, as a 2×15 contingency table, we can test the null hypothesis that the patterns within each table are the same with a χ^2 test with 14 degrees of freedom. The likelihood ratio χ^2 = 9.21; P = .82. We cannot reject the null hypothesis. Intraclass correlations for Tables 1a and 1b are .069 and .067, respectively. The difference is not statistically significant (Z = .05, P = .96). With a sample of over 2000 twins and probabilities this size, it is quite clear that if there is any difference between the two patterns, it must be rather small. This is true whether we consider a generalised test for any difference (χ^2) or a specific test of correlation between siblings (intraclass r). However, we do not have adequate power to detect differences in proportion of concordance of the order of .02, which some genetic models would predict. Even larger samples than this would be required to test such hypotheses adequately.

It seems quite justifiable to merge the two tables for further hypothesis testing. The null hypothesis that handedness in twin pairs is not correlated was then tested. If $P(i)$ is the probability that any individual twin falls in category i; then under the null hypothesis of independence, the probability that both members of a pair fall in category i is $P(i)^2$ and the probability that one member falls in i and the other in j is $2[P(i) P(j)]$. The merged data, the expected values of the merged data under the null hypothesis, and the maximum likelihood estimators of the $P(i)$s are presented in Table 2.

TABLE 1a
Pairwise Concordance for DZ Twins

	Strong Left	Weak Left	Ambidextrous	Weak Right	Strong Right
Str. L	6 (.006)				
Weak L	1 (.001)	1 (.001)			
Ambi-	3 (.003)	1 (.001)	1 (.001)		
Weak R	6 (.006)	3 (.003)	9 (.009)	18 (.018)	
Str. R	65 (.067)	28 (.029)	44 (.045)	157 (.161)	630 (.647)

N = 973
Intraclass r = .069

TABLE 1b
Pairwise Concordance for MZ Twins

	Strong Left	Weak Left	Ambidextrous	Weak Right	Strong Right
Str. L	6 (.005)				
Weak L	6 (.005)	1 (.001)			
Ambi-	2 (.002)	3 (.003)	3 (.003)		
Weak R	10 (.009)	5 (.004)	10 (.009)	20 (.017)	
Str. R	88 (.076)	32 (.028)	69 (.060)	185 (.160)	718 (.620)

N = 1158
Intraclass r = .067
χ^2 = 9.21; P = .82

TABLE 2
Total Pairwise Concordance for Twins

	Strong Left	Weak Left	Ambidextrous	Weak Right	Strong Right
Observed					
Str. L	12				
Weak L	7	2			
Ambi-	5	4	4		
Weak R	16	8	19	38	
Str. R	153	60	113	342	1348
Expected Under Null Hypothesis					
Str. L	4.93				
Weak L	3.99	.81			
Ambi-	7.17	2.90	2.60		
Weak	22.17	8.98	16.12	24.93	
Str. R	161.81	65.51	117.61	363.87	1327.60
Est. *P*	.048	.019	.035	.108	.789

$\chi^2 = 23.24; P < .01$

As 5 parameters are fit under the null hypothesis and 15 are fit when each cell is allowed its own probability, we can test whether the full model fits better then the independence model with a χ^2 test with 10 df. The likelihood ratio $\chi^2 = 24.00; P < .01$. We can reject the null hypothesis. We can see in Table 2 that all of the diagonal entries, which represent both twins being in the same category, have an excess of entries, and that three of the four subdiagonal categories, which represent the members of a pair being one category removed from each other, have an excess of entries. The other cells all have a deficit. This indicates that there is some degree of positive correlation in handedness. Consideration that the observed proportion of agreement is .66 while the proportion expected by chance is .64, it has to be concluded that the effect, although statistically significant, is small.

Unconfounding Direction and Consistency of Handedness

For the concordance analyses just described, the resultant single score per subject confounds the consistency and direction factors. Recall that the continuous laterality criterion was collapsed into five arbitrary categories: Strong Left, Weak Left, Ambidextrous, Weak Right, and Strong Right.

For the pure consistency analysis (Table 3a), Ambidextrous remained the same, whereas Weak Left and Weak Right were merged, as were Strong Left and Strong Right, to yield three consistency categories independent of direction.

TABLE 3a
Pairwise Concordance for Consistency of Handedness

	DZ			MZ			SUM		
	S	W	A	S	W	A	S	W	A
S	701			812			1513		
W	192	22		233	26		425	48	
A	47	10	1	71	13	3	118	23	4
Expected Under Null Hypothesis									
S	691.9			802.5			1494.3		
W	207.4	15.6		248.1	19.2		455.6	34.7	
A	49.7	7.5	.9	74.9	11.6	1.7	124.8	19.0	2.6

$N = 2131$

We found no significant difference between the MZ and DZ Tables ($\chi^2_{(5)} = 2.72$, $P = .74$). As likelihood ratio chi squares are additive and 2.72 would not be statistically significant with even one degree of freedom, we can conclude that there is no single degree of freedom contrast between the tables that would be statistically significant. However, within the combined MZ + DZ Table, the null hypothesis of independence was rejected ($\chi^2_{(3)} = 8.68$, $P = .03$). The frequencies in the diagonal cells exceed chance expectation. Thus, there was significant pairwise concordance for consistency of handedness irrespective of direction. Associated intraclass correlations: .058 for MZ; .052 for DZ; and .055 for the combined Table.

For the pure directional analysis (Table 3b), 14 pairs in which at least one member had a Bryden score of zero were dropped. We then combined all negative Bryden scores as Left and all positive Bryden scores as Right to yield two directional categories, independent of consistency. The difference between the MZ and DZ Tables was again nonsignificant ($\chi^2_{(2)} = 2.76$, $P = .25$). The

TABLE 3b
Pairwise Concordance for Direction of Handedness

	DZ		MZ		SUM	
	L	R	L	R	L	R
L	11		17		28	
R	128	826	179	956	307	1782
Expected Under Null Hypothesis						
L	5.8		9.8		15.6	
R	138.3	820.8	193.3	948.8	331.9	1769.6

$N = 2117$

frequencies in the diagonal cells exceed chance expectation. Again, we can conclude that there is no statistically significant contrast between the tables. Within the combined Table, the null hypothesis of independence was again rejected ($\chi^2_{(1)}$ = 10.02, P = .002). Thus, there was also significant concordance for direction of handedness irrespective of consistency. Associated intraclass correlations: .076 for MZ; .09 for DZ; and .086 for the combined Table.

Structural Equations Model

We attempted to fit structural equation models for both consistency and direction of handedness. For consistency of handedness, we found statistically significant effects for common environment, but not for genetics. Specifically, the best fitting model for consistency of handedness (goodness of fit $\chi^2_{(11)}$ = 8.75, P = .64) estimated that 12.0% of the covariance of liability in consistency of handedness was attributable to common environment and the remaining 88.0% to unique environment. Although the best fitting model for direction of handedness contained the same terms for common environment and unique environment, there was a statistically significant lack of fit (goodness of fit $\chi^2_{(3)}$ = 8.728, P = .03). Thus, no structural equations model adequately fits the data on direction of handedness, although the best fitting model estimated that roughly 20% of the covariance of liability in consistency of handedness was attributable to common environment and the rest to unique environment.

DISCUSSION

No zygosity differences were found in this study. However, from the pooled MZ/DZ data, both for the raw laterality index (which confounds consistency and direction), and for the two factors separately, we conclude that concordance is greater than would be predicted if the handedness of members of a twin pair were independent. The incidence of sinistrality in the population is known to increase as "right-handed world" pressure declines. Problems due to this bias are described in Salive, Guralnil, and Glynn (1993).

Our structural equations model results were in accord with the simple chi-square analyses in showing that common environment, rather than genetics, affects consistency and direction of handedness. For consistency of handedness, the structural equations model estimated that 12% of twin variability is attributable to common environment, and the rest to unique environment; specifically, genetic effects were not significant. A similar model for direction of handedness showed significant lack of fit, but again the best fitting model attributed twin variability to the effects of common and unique environment, rather than genetics.

The conjecture of a gene for consistency of laterality that cannot distinguish left from right derives from animal studies showing that mice can be bred for strength but not for direction of "pawedness" (Collins, 1977, 1991).

Lateralisation of paw usage in the laboratory mouse is a useful model system for assessing expression and biological causes of development asymmetries. Thus, in a study of 12 inbred strains, Biddle et al. (1993) found that degree of lateralisation fell into two groups of highly and weakly lateralised paw preference, suggesting that "a major gene may control some function and alternate alleles are expressed as weakly lateralized and highly lateralized paw preference" (Biddle & Eales, 1996, p. 392). This hypothesis was made "more plausible by considering that the highly lateralized groups of strains may be similar to the HI and LO phenotypes that were selected by Collins" (Biddle & Eales, 1996, p. 392). But Biddle and Eales (1996) subsequently reported an expanded study of genetically different strains and stocks of the laboratory mouse, including different species and subspecies. The major genetic trait was degree of lateralisation of paw preference and the strain differences appeared to fall into three major classes of highly lateralised, weakly lateralised, and ambilateral preference. Some strains appeared to exhibit a directional deviation from equal numbers of mice with left and right paw usage, suggesting that direction may not be a genetically neutral trait. The investigators added that replicate assessments and genetic tests were needed to confirm this. They also noted that in some strains, "paw usage may be two separate traits of direction and degree of lateralization" as "there was evidence of significant deviation of the numbers of mice to the left and right of equal paw usage that is independent of the degree of lateralization" (Biddle & Eales, 1996, p. 392). Thus, the field remains controversial (McManus, 1992; Collins, Sargent, & Neumann, 1993).

We found concordance for consistency irrespective of direction, and for direction irrespective of consistency in the combined table. This, plus the absence of zygosity differences between the separate tables, underscores McManus' (1980, p. 347) remark that "twin studies are the Achilles' heel of handedness genetics." Our result does not resolve this point in humans.

Manuscript received 17 April 1997
Revised manuscript received 11 September 1998

REFERENCES

Biddle, F.G., Coffaro, C.M., Ziehr, J.E., & Eales, B.A. (1993). Genetic variation in paw preference (handedness) in the mouse. *Genome*, *36*, 935–943.

Biddle, F.G., & Eales, B.A. (1996). The degree of lateralization of paw usage (handedness) in the mouse is defined by three major phenotypes. [In M. Carlier (Ed.), Special Issue on Genetics and Laterality] *Behavioral Genetics*, *26*, 391–406.

Bryden, M.P. (1982). *Laterality: Functional asymmetry in the intact brain*. New York, Academic Press.

Collins, R.L. (1977). Origins of the sense of asymmetry: Mendelian and non-Mendelian models of inheritance. In S.J. Dimond & D.A. Blizard (Eds.), *Evolution and lateralization of the brain. Annals of the New York Academy of Science*, *299*, 283–305.

Collins, R.L. (1991). Reimpressed selective breeding for lateralization of handedness in mice. *Brain Research, 564,* 194–202.

Collins, R.L., Sargent, E.E., & Neumann, P.E. (1993). Genetic and behavioural tests of the McManus hypothesis relating response to selection for lateralization of handedness in mice to degree of heterozygosity. *Behavioural Genetics, 23,* 413–421.

Kendler, K.S., Heath, A.C., Neale, M.C., Kessler, R.C., & Eaves, L.J. (1992). A population based twin study of alcoholism in women. *Journal of the American Medical Association, 268,* 1877–1882.

McManus, I.C. (1980). Handedness in twins: A critical review. *Neuropsychologia, 18,* 347–355.

McManus, I.C. (1992). Are paw preference differences in HI and LO mice the result of specific genes or of heterosis and fluctuating asymmetry? *Behavioral Genetics, 22,* 435–451.

Neale, M.C. & Cardon, L.R. (1992). *Methodology for genetic studies of twins and families.* Boston: Kluwer Academic Publishers.

Salive, M.E., Guralnik, J.M., & Glynn, R.J. (1993). Left-handedness and mortality. *American Journal of Public Health, 83,* 265–267.

LATERALITY, 1999, 4 (3), 265–286

Handedness in Twins: A Meta-analysis

Nancy L. Sicotte, Roger P. Woods and John C. Mazziotta

UCLA School of Medicine, USA

In the largest meta-analysis of twins and singletons conducted to date we have found a higher incidence of left-handedness in twins compared to singletons. Our analysis revealed no difference in the frequency of left-handedness among monozygotic versus dizygotic twins. However, identical twins were more likely to be concordant for hand preference than non-identical twins, which is consistent with a genetic model of handedness. Prior analyses have not revealed these findings consistently, and this has led to a number of conflicting models of handedness.

INTRODUCTION

An overwhelming majority of humans prefer to use their right hand for most tasks. A small but significant minority of individuals in all cultures identify themselves as left-handed or ambidextrous (Hecaen & Ajuriaguerra, 1964). This simple but striking observation has generated much speculation but remains unexplained. The tantalising relationship between hand preference and cerebral dominance for language has fuelled attempts to characterise the biology of handedness. Anomalous language lateralisation is more common in left-handers (Hecaen, Da Agostini, & Monzon-Montes, 1981), and it has been reported that aphasics with a family history of left-handedness show less severe deficits and better recovery than those without familial sinistrality, even if they themselves are right-handed (Luria, 1970; Subirana, 1958).

Whether variations in hand preference are determined genetically, environmentally, as a result of cultural bias, or some combination of these remains controversial (Annett, 1985; Collins, 1970; Laland, Kumm, Van Horn, &

Requests for reprints should be sent to Nancy Sicotte MD, Department of Neurology, UCLA School of Medicine, 710 Westwood Plaza, Los Angeles, CA 90095, USA.

The work was supported by the Dorothy B. and Leonard Straus Fund for Scholars in Neuroscience, National Institute of Neurological Disorders and Stroke Grant 1 K08 NS-01646, and generous gifts from the Pierson–Lovelace Foundation, The Ahmanson Foundation, and the Brain Mapping Medical Research Organization.

The authors would like to thank Dan Geschwind and Marco Iacoboni for their helpful comments regarding this manuscript.

Feldman, 1995; McManus, 1985). Handedness does run in families. Offspring of left-handed parents are three to ten times more likely to be left-handed than the offspring of two right-handed parents (Chamberlain, 1928; Coren, 1992; McManus & Bryden, 1992; Rife, 1940). These results, although interesting, are inconclusive; they are consistent with either a genetic or an environmental model of handedness. Only a few adoption studies addressing the issue of handedness have been done, but they suggest that non-biological parents' hand preference has little influence on adoptees' handedness, which is consistent with a genetic theory (Carter-Saltzman, 1980; Hicks & Kinsbourne, 1976). A classic approach to the nature versus nurture question has been the twin study. Beginning with Galton (1875) many investigators have compared monozygotic and dizygotic twins to determine the relative importance of genetic and/or environmental influences for a variety of traits. Not surprisingly, this method has been popular in the study of handedness. However, the results of these studies are, perhaps, surprising. Even among identical twins, frequently one twin is right-handed and the other is left-handed. Discordant handedness is also very common among non-identical twins. Simple Mendelian genetic models defining right-and left-handedness as recessive or dominant traits cannot account for this pattern of findings, leading many researchers to argue that variations in handedness are determined solely by parental and cultural influences (Laland et al., 1995; Tambs, Magnus, & Berg, 1987) or by biological influences such as hormones or position in the womb (Geschwind & Galaburda, 1985).

A confounding factor may be that twins are not representative of the population as a whole. Many studies have suggested that twins have a higher incidence of left-handedness than their singleton counterparts (Davis & Annett, 1994; Rife, 1940; Williams et al., Buss, & Eskenazi, 1992), though others have not (Ellis, Ellis, & Marshall, 1988; Morley & Caffrey, 1994; von Verschuer, 1927). The possible explanations for this finding are numerous. Twins are at greater risk for perinatal morbidity and mortality, and they are frequently born prematurely. A history of birth stress has been associated with a higher incidence of left-handedness (Bakan, 1971; Williams et al, 1992) and left-handedness is much more common among neurologically impaired individuals (Dellatolas et al., 1993; Gordon, 1921; Satz, Orsini, Saslow, & Henry, 1985). Others have suggested that the twinning process itself is pathological (Corballis & Morgan, 1978; James, 1983). Investigators from the early part of this century popularised a theory to explain the excess left-handedness and frequent discordance in monozygotic twins. Known as "mirror imaging", this theory postulated that identical twins represented "right" and "left" halves of a single egg (Newman, 1928; Stocks, 1933). This theory continues to be used to interpret discordant handedness in monozygotic twins (Davis & Phelps, 1995; Davis, Phelps, & Bracha, 1995).

A critical look at the twin data may help to clarify some of these issues. If the incidence of left-handedness is similar in monozygotic and dizygotic twins, then mirror imaging as an explanation is eliminated. One could then compare the differences in the proportions of discordant to concordant pairs among monozygotic and dizygotic twins. If handedness is genetic, as the family data would suggest, then monozygotic twins should be more likely to have similar handedness, i.e. more right–right and left–left pairs than their dizygotic counterparts. Some previous reviews of twin data have found this to be the case (McManus, 1980; McManus & Bryden, 1992; Zazzo, 1960). From the literature we have gathered the largest number of twin pairs to date and applied new statistical analyses to answer three straightforward questions that remain controversial:

1. Is there a difference in the incidence of left-handedness in twins compared to singletons?
2. Is there a difference in the incidence of left-handedness between monozygotic and dizygotic twins?
3. Is there a difference in the concordance for left-handedness in monozygotic versus dizygotic twins?

The answers to these questions have important implications for the study of human handedness.

METHOD

A review of the literature was performed using *Melvyl MEDLINE* (1966–present) and *Psychological Abstracts* (1966–present) with the keywords "twins" and "handedness". The resulting articles were obtained and references searched for pertinent articles. Original articles cited in prior reviews (Laland et al., 1995; McManus, 1985; Nagylaki & Levy, 1973; Zazzo, 1960) were obtained. All studies with at least 10 twin pairs were considered. Studies had to include at least two groups of subjects, either monozygotic and dizygotic twins, or twins and singletons. Studies of only monozygotic twins, or studies that included twins with psychopathology or obvious neurological impairment were excluded. Table 1 shows details of the studies used. Table 2 shows details of studies that were excluded for the various reasons cited.

Handedness was determined in many different ways as detailed in Table 1. Most studies assigned individuals as either right-handed or left-handed. In some studies, ambidextrous individuals were identified but then combined with another group by the original investigators (see Table 1 for details). In the few cases where the numbers of ambidextrous individuals were reported individually, we combined them with the left-handers for consistency with the majority of studies and with prior reviews. Zygosity was most frequently determined by questionnaire and/or physical similarities. Blood antigen testing was performed in some smaller studies and within subgroups of some larger studies.

TABLE 1
Summary of Studies Used for Analysis

Author(s)	Date	Twin Pairs	Singletons	Handedness Criteria	Zygosity Criteria
Siemens	1924	82	0	not stated	similarities
Dahlberg	1926	197	0	throwing hand, cutting hand	similarities
von Verschuer	1927	117	566	not stated	similarities
Hirsch	1930	101	0	self report	similarities
Wilson & Jones	1932	193	521	throwing hand	similarities
Stocks	1933	136	156	writing; ambidextrous = R	similarities
Komai & Fukuoka	1934a,b	180	16267	writing brush	similarities
Newman, Freeman & Holzinger	1937	100	0	finger tapping	similarities
Rife	1940	369	3542	left = any task w/left	not stated
Thyss	1946	189	0	unknown	unknown
Rife	1950	554	0	left = any task w/left	not stated
Dechaume	1957	66	0	unknown	unknown
Zazzo	1960	594	0	self report	similarities
Koch	1966	90	0	observation/parental report	similarities
Carter-Saltzman et al.	1976	363	0	writing; ambidextrous = L	blood typing
Loehlin & Nichols	1976	847	0	self rating	questionnaire
Springer & Searleman	1978	122	0	writing hand	blood typing
Hay & Howie	1980	29	0	manual tasks	blood typing
Osborne	1980	237	0	self report	questionnaire
Boklage	1981	428	0	self report	questionnaire
Shimizu & Endo	1983	110	4282	questionnaire	parental report
Forrai & Bankovi	1983	164	0	self report	blood typing
Tambs et al.	1987	400	858	writing hand	questionnaire
NCDS*	unpub	131	0	writing hand	similarities
Neale	1988	1668	0	self report; ambidextrous = L	questionnaire
Williams et al.	1992	70†	5845	writing; ambidextrous excluded	not characterised
Ellis	1988	119†	5978	Edinburgh Inventory	not characterised
Davis & Annett	1994	902†	32499	writing hand	not characterised
Coren	1994	298†	1192	Lateral Preference Inventory	not characterised
Morley & Caffrey	1994	102†	3694	writing hand	not characterised
Derom et al.	1996	760	0	self report	blood typing
Carlier et al.	1996	79	0	writing hand	DNA analysis
Orlebeke et al.	1996	1663	0	self report	questionnaire

* as cited by McManus
† Twin individuals not pairs

TABLE 2
Studies Excluded From Analyses

Author(s)	Date	Reason for exclusion
Weitz	1924	MZ twins only
Lauterbach	1925	No zygosity information
Bouterwek	1938	Incorrect reference cited in Zazzo, unable to find correct reference
Shields	1962	Pair-wise data not given
Teng, Lee, Young & Chang	1976	Individual handedness not reported
Springer & Searleman	1978	Only right-handed twins studied
Clark, Klouoff & Tyhurst	1986	MZ twins only
Liebing	1986	Exact numbers of twins used not clear
Segal	1989	Full data reported on MZ twins only
Gilger et al.	1992	Pair-wise data not given
Jäncke & Steinmetz	1994	MZ twins only
Perelle & Ehrman	1994	Unable to determine exact numbers of twins studied, no pair-wise data given

A total of 33 studies were included for analysis. Of these, 16 have been included in earlier meta-analyses and reviews cited previously; 12 included data on singletons and twins ascertained in the same manner; 5 did not provide information regarding zygosity and are used only in the twin/singleton analysis. A total of 28 studies were analysed that included handedness and zygosity information for a total of 9969 twin pairs (see Table 3). These data were analysed two ways: as individuals ($n = 19,938$) to compare overall handedness in monozygotic and dizygotic twins, and as pairs ($n = 9969$) to compare concordant/discordant handedness in monozygotic and dizygotic twins. Two by two contingency tables were constructed to allow three primary analyses and one secondary analysis:

1. Twin status (twin or singleton) by handedness, to test the hypothesis that left-handedness is increased among twins.

2. Zygosity by handedness, to test the hypothesis that left-handedness is more common among monozygotic twins as predicted by ''mirror imaging'' hypotheses.

3. Zygosity by concordance for left-handedness, to test the hypothesis that having a left-handed monozygotic twin increases the likelihood of being left-handed more than having a left-handed dizygotic twin (right–right twin pairs were excluded for this analysis leaving only right–left and left–left pairs).

4. A secondary analysis of zygosity by concordance for handedness, to test the hypothesis that monozygotic twins are more likely than dizygotic twins to be concordant for handedness (right–right and left–left pairs were classified as concordant, right–left pairs as discordant). This was classified as a secondary

TABLE 3
Summary of Handedness Distribution in Twin Pairs

Author(s)	Date	MZ			DZ		
		RR	RL	LL	RR	RL	LL
Siemens	1924	41	9	1	16	13	2
Dahlberg	1926	53	12	4	111	16	1
von Verschuer	1927	58	15	6	28	10	0
Hirsch	1930	25	18	0	51	7	0
Wilson & Jones	1932	56	13	1	97	24	2
Stocks	1933	35	6	1	76	16	2
Komai & Fukuska	1934a	112	6	0	60	1	1
Newman et al.	1937	30	17	3	39	11	0
Rife	1940	176	41	6	104	39	3
Thyss	1946	72	24	7	60	24	2
Rife	1950	261	76	6	164	45	2
Dechaume	1957	19	12	2	21	11	1
Zazzo	1960	199	51	9	264	69	2
Koch	1966	28	3	4	45	6	4
Carter-Saltzmann et al.	1976	132	46	9	115	54	7
Loehlin & Nichols	1976	380	123	11	261	70	2
Springer & Searleman	1978	53	19	3	35	9	3
Hay & Howie	1980	9	7	0	10	3	0
Osborne	1980	76	27	4	90	40	0
Boklage	1981	145	45	24	132	69	13
Shimizu & Endo	1983	57	4	1	41	7	0
Forrai & Bankovi	1983	78	16	2	44	21	3
Tambs et al.	1987	175	21	1	171	32	0
NCDs*	unpub	32	9	2	66	18	4
Neale	1988	655	158	23	626	183	23
Derom et al.	1996	249	86	17	276	109	23
Carlier et al.	1996	48	6	1	15	9	0
Orlebeke et al.	1996	475	122	25	764	255	22

* as cited by McManus

hypothesis because it is correlated with the previous analysis, differing only by the addition of the right–right pairs. Both pertain to the issue of genetic influences in determining handedness.

Odds ratios (OR) and corresponding two-tailed 95% confidence intervals were calculated for each study independently. Two-tailed P-values were also computed individually for each study and again across all studies for the null hypothesis that the odds ratio was equal to 1, as described in detail next. The logarithms of the upper and lower confidence intervals for the odds ratio were calculated and graphed for each individual study.

TABLE 4
Odds Ratio, 95% Confidence Intervals (CIs), and P-values from Twin/Singleton Analysis
(Log CIs Used in Graph)

| | Twins/Singletons | | Left vs Right | | |
Author	Date	OR	CI-upper	CI-lower	P-value
von Verschuer	1927	1.01	1.55	0.64	1.00E+00
Wilson & Jones	1932	1.80	2.97	1.09	1.58E−02
Stocks	1933	2.44	6.78	1.01	4.28E−02
Komai & Fukuoka	1934a,b	2.22	4.35	0.99	4.01E−02
Rife	1940	1.91	2.46	1.48	8.72E−07
Shimizu & Endo	1983	1.90	3.43	0.97	4.99E−02
Tambs et al.	1987	1.50	2.35	0.96	7.36E−02
Ellis et al.	1988	1.32	2.43	0.66	3.87E−01
Williams et al.	1992	2.38	4.30	1.24	5.32E−03
Davis & Annett	1994	1.72	2.13	1.39	1.22E−06
Coren	1994	1.53	2.26	1.03	2.83E−02
Morley & Caffrey	1994	1.09	1.97	0.55	7.56E−01

Statistical analyses of the 2×2 contingency tables were performed using Fisher's exact method and an analogous extension of this method applicable to multiple 2×2 tables (Gart, 1970; Mehta, 1994). Unlike chi-square methods, which become unreliable as the number of observations in any row or column becomes small, exact test results are reliable in all cases. For a single 2×2 table, the method is based on the assumption that the totals for each row and column of the table are fixed (e.g. for an analysis of handedness versus zygosity, that the total number of left-handers, total number of right-handers, total number of monozygotic twins, and total number of dizygotic twins is fixed). Under this assumption, the observed value for any single cell suffices to determine the values that must be present in all of the other cells. For any given value of the odds ratio, the value predicted for a given cell can be calculated. For example, for an odds ratio of 1 (the null hypothesis in all cases described here), the most likely value for the first cell is the product of the likelihood of appearing in the first row multiplied by the likelihood of appearing in the first column. Starting with the first whole number higher than this most likely value, the probabilities of obtaining increasingly higher values become progressively lower. Similarly, starting with the first whole number lower than this most likely value, the probabilities of obtaining increasingly lower values become progressively lower. For each whole number value in the first cell, a probability of observing that value under the assumption of a particular value for the odds ratio can be computed exactly. All of these probabilities must sum to unity. The exact two-tailed P value associated with a given value in the first cell can be obtained by adding all individual probabilities that are less than or equal to the observed value in either tail (the probability of the observed value is also included in this

TABLE 5
Data From MZ/DZ Individuals Analysis. Log CIs Used in Graph

| Author | MZ and DZ | | Left vs Right | | |
	Date	OR	CI-upper	CI-lower	P-value
Siemens	1924	0.32	0.80	0.13	9.45E−03
Dahlberg	1926	2.24	4.67	1.08	2.02E−02
von Verschuer	1927	1.36	3.34	0.59	5.66E−01
Hirsch	1930	4.12	12.23	1.53	2.10E−03
Wilson & Jones	1932	0.93	1.89	0.45	1.00E+00
Stocks	1933	0.88	2.21	0.32	1.00E+00
Komai & Fukuoka	1934a	1.05	6.61	0.22	1.00E+00
Newman et al.	1937	2.42	5.84	1.05	3.73E−02
Rife	1940	0.74	1.17	0.47	1.84E−01
Thyss	1946	1.16	2.07	0.66	5.90E−01
Rife	1950	1.12	1.66	0.76	5.74E−01
Dechaume	1957	1.30	3.27	0.53	6.75E−01
Zazzo	1960	1.26	1.81	0.87	2.08E−01
Koch	1966	1.28	3.26	0.49	6.60E−01
Carter-Saltzmann et al.	1976	0.86	1.28	0.58	4.43E−01
Loehlin & Nichols	1976	1.31	1.80	0.97	7.55E−02
Springer & Searleman	1978	1.05	2.29	0.50	1.00E+00
Hay & Howie	1980	2.15	14.21	0.42	4.87E−01
Osborne	1980	1.08	1.82	0.63	8.01E−01
Boklage	1981	0.97	1.36	0.69	9.34E−01
Shimizu & Endo	1983	0.65	2.34	0.17	5.67E−01
Forrai & Bankovi	1983	0.47	0.92	0.24	2.43E−02
Tambs et al.	1987	0.72	1.31	0.40	2.67E−01
NCDS*	unpub	1.03	2.22	0.46	1.00E+00
Neale	1988	0.87	1.07	0.71	1.81E−01
Derom et al.	1996	0.88	1.15	0.67	3.50E−01
Carlier et al.	1996	0.34	1.08	0.11	4.83E−02
Orlebeke et al.	1996	0.96	1.18	0.78	6.81E−01

* as cited by McManus

sum). This is analogous to integrating the area in the two tails of a probability distribution, but can be done by simple addition due to the exact nature of the test. One-tailed analyses include only the values from the appropriate tail and 95% confidence intervals can be computed by determining the odds ratio that results in a one-tailed P value of 0.025.

Meta-analysis of multiple 2×2 contingency tables is accomplished by an analogous procedure. It is again assumed that the number of observations in the rows and columns of each individual 2×2 table is fixed. Although irrelevent to the analysis, this also means that the number of observations in the rows and columns of a grand total summary table would remain fixed. However, relying solely on a grand summary table ignores information contained within the

TABLE 6
Data From MZ/DZ Twin Pair Analysis (LL/RL). Log CIs Used in Graph

Author	MZ and DZ			LL vs RL		
	Date	OR		CI-Upper	CI-lower	P-value
Siemens	1924	0.72		16.12	0.01	1.00E+00
Dahlberg	1926	5.33		278.70	0.43	1.75E−01
von Verschuer	1927	infinity		infinity	0.61	1.41E−01
Hirsch	1930	0.00		infinity	0.00	1.00E+00
Wilson & Jones	1932	0.92		19.38	0.01	1.00E+00
Stocks	1933	1.33		29.99	0.02	1.00E+00
Komai & Fukuoka	1934a	0.00		13.00	0.00	2.50E−01
Newman et al.	1937	infinity		infinity	0.23	5.35E−01
Rife	1940	1.90		12.48	0.37	4.91E−01
Thyss	1946	3.50		37.50	0.57	1.60E−01
Rife	1950	1.78		18.65	0.30	7.10E−01
Dechaume	1957	1.83		117.84	0.08	1.00E+00
Zazzo	1960	6.09		59.52	1.17	2.29E−02
Koch	1966	2.00		21.62	0.19	6.37E−01
Carter-Saltzmann et al.	1976	1.51		5.16	0.46	5.91E−01
Loehlin & Nichols	1976	3.13		29.73	0.65	1.47E−01
Springer & Searleman	1978	0.47		4.36	0.05	6.41E−01
Hay & Howie	1980	0.00		infinity	0.00	1.00E+00
Osborne	1980	infinity		infinity	0.89	3.24E−02
Boklage	1981	2.83		6.68	1.23	8.19E−03
Shimizu & Endo	1983	infinity		infinity	0.40	4.17E−01
Forrai & Bankovi	1983	0.88		8.64	0.07	1.00E+00
Tambs et al.	1987	infinity		infinity	0.04	4.07E−01
NCDS*	unpub	1.00		8.64	0.08	1.00E+00
Neale	1988	1.16		2.25	0.60	6.41E−01
Derom et al.	1996	0.94		1.96	0.44	1.00E+00
Carlier et al.	1996	infinity		infinity	0.03	4.38E−01
Orlebeke et al.	1996	2.38		4.61	1.23	5.79E−03

* as cited by McManus

individual tables and is inappropriate for meta-analysis. Instead, the grand total of the values in the first cell of all the tables is used as the basis for analysis. Under the assumption of a common odds ratio shared by all tables, the probabilities of all possible arrangements of values within each of the individual tables are computed. These probabilities are then used to compute the exact probability of the observed grand total value. It can be shown mathematically that the result is independent of which cell is chosen to compute the grand total. Exact P values and 95% confidence intervals can then be calculated in a manner analogous to their computation in a single 2×2 table. Computation is mathematically straightforward but computationally intensive. The validity of the calculations can be verified by showing that the

TABLE 7
Data From MZ/DZ Twin Pair Analysis (RR + LL)/RL. Log CIs Used in Graph

| Author | MZ and DZ | | (RR + LL)/RL | | |
	Date	OR	CI-upper	CI-lower	P-value
Siemens	1924	3.37	10.58	1.09	2.15E−02
Dahlberg	1926	0.68	1.69	0.28	3.94E−01
von Verschuer	1927	1.52	4.14	0.54	4.70E−01
Hirsch	1930	0.19	0.56	0.06	9.25E−04
Wilson & Jones	1932	1.06	2.46	0.48	1.00E+00
Stocks	1933	1.23	4.16	0.41	8.04E−01
Komai & Fukuoka	1934a	0.31	2.63	0.01	4.25E−01
Newman et al.	1937	0.55	1.45	0.20	2.65E−01
Rife	1940	1.62	2.75	0.95	7.03E−02
Thyss	1946	1.27	2.59	0.63	5.05E−01
Rife	1950	0.95	1.47	0.61	8.33E−01
Dechaume	1957	0.88	2.71	0.28	1.00E+00
Zazzo	1960	1.06	1.62	0.69	8.37E−01
Koch	1966	1.31	8.62	0.26	1.00E+00
Carter-Saltzmann et al.	1976	1.36	2.21	0.83	1.99E−01
Loehlin & Nichols	1976	0.85	1.19	0.60	3.57E−01
Springer & Searleman	1978	0.70	1.83	0.25	5.10E−01
Hay & Howie	1980	0.39	2.45	0.05	4.33E−01
Osborne	1980	1.32	2.44	0.72	3.86E−01
Boklage	1981	1.79	2.84	1.13	1.17E−02
Shimizu & Endo	1983	2.48	12.21	0.58	2.05E−01
Forrai & Bankovi	1983	2.23	5.05	1.00	3.79E−02
Tambs et al.	1987	1.57	2.98	0.84	1.42E−01
NCDS*	unpub	0.97	2.72	0.37	1.00E+00
Neale	1988	1.21	1.55	0.95	1.29E−01
Derom et al.	1996	1.13	1.59	0.80	5.06E−01
Carlier et al.	1996	4.90	19.30	1.28	1.07E−02
Orlebeke et al.	1996	1.33	1.71	1.03	2.16E−02

* as cited by McManus

sum of all possible values for the selected cell is unity, or by interchanging rows or columns.

This method of meta-analysis has several advantages for analysis of twin and handedness data. First, as the number of left-handers is often small, the exact test eliminates concerns about the validity of approximations made with inexact methods. A second advantage is that studies of different sizes can be combined appropriately, because the influences of larger and smaller studies are balanced automatically and exactly. A third advantage is that when the null hypothesis is a common odds ratio of unity, meta-analytic rejection of this particular null hypothesis is valid even if the true odds ratio varies across studies (e.g. due to variations in handedness definition or to variations in the frequency of left-handedness). It is possible that the true odds ratios from different studies will differ, so 95% confidence intervals for a hypothetical common odds radio are of dubious value. Likewise, failure to reject the null hypothesis for the meta-analysis of all studies should be augmented with consideration of each individual study (with appropriate adjustment for the fact that this requires testing of multiple hypotheses) before accepting the null hypothesis. In both of these later situations, plots of the 95% confidence intervals for each individual study provide a visual means for assessing the consistency of the various results. As odds ratios of 0.5 and 2.0 represent equivalent deviations from the null hypothesis, use of the logarithm of the odds ratio provides a neutral assessment of the null hypothesis. A positive logarithm represents a deviation from this null hypothesis in one direction and a negative logarithm of the same magnitude represents an equivalent deviation in the opposite direction.

RESULTS

Figure 1 shows the log confidence intervals for the 12 studies that included data needed to investigate the relationship between twin status (twin or singleton) and handedness. Considered individually, four of the twelve studies fail to reject the two-tailed null hypothesis of an odds ratio of 1. The remaining eight studies all individually support the hypothesis that left-handedness is more common among twins. When the studies are combined, the null hypothesis of a common odds ratio of 1 is rejected with a two-tailed P-value of 8.8×10^{-17}. None of the individual studies shows results indicating that left-handedness is *less* common in twins.

Figure 2 shows the results for handedness as a function of zygosity for each study. The results do not support the hypothesis that monozygotic and dizygotic twins have different frequencies of left-handedness. The estimated common odds ratio across all studies was 0.99 and did not differ significantly from an odds ratio of 1 ($P = 0.75$), indicating that the overall incidence of left-handedness is the same in both twin groups. A few individual outliers include earlier studies by Siemens (1924) and Hirsch (1930) although in opposite directions.

Figures 3 and 4 show the results of the twin pair analyses. Figure 3 shows the results of the concordant left (LL) by discordant (RL) analyses. In the group analysis the number of LL pairs is significantly higher among monozygotic twin pairs as compared to dizygotic twin pairs ($P = 2.7 \times 10^{-6}$). An analysis of a subgroup of same-sex only pairs does not alter this finding ($P = 8.6 \times 10^{-4}$). To further demonstrate this relationship, the total concordant pairs (RR + LL) were compared to the discordant pairs (RL) for both twin types as shown in Fig. 4. The results are still significant ($P = 6.7 \times 10^{-4}$) and demonstrate a higher frequency of concordant monozygotic pairs than dizygotic pairs.

276

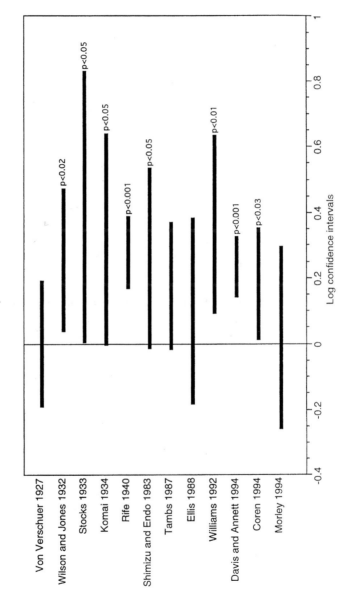

FIG. 1. Log 95% confidence intervals of odds ratios determined for the 12 studies comparing handedness in twins and singletons. Positive values indicate increased left-handedness in twins.

MZ and DZ Individuals

Zygosity by Handedness

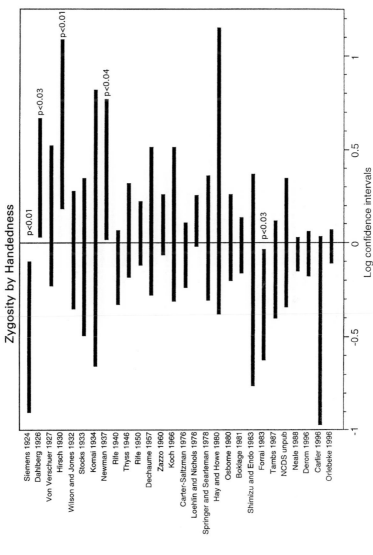

FIG. 2. Log 95% confidence intervals of odds ratio for the 28 studies comparing handedness in monozygotic and dizygotic individuals. Positive values indicate increased left-handedness in monozygotic individuals.

278

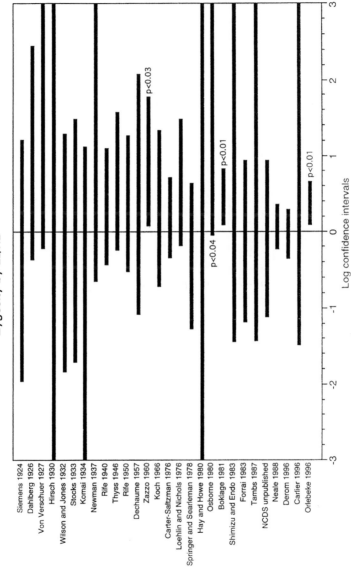

MZ and DZ Pairs

Zygosity by LL/RL

FIG. 3. Log 95% confidence intervals of odds ratios for the 28 studies comparing discordant (RL) and concordant (LL) twin pairs. Positive values indicate increased left–left pairs in monozygotic twins.

MZ and DZ Pairs

Zygosity by (RR + LL)/RL

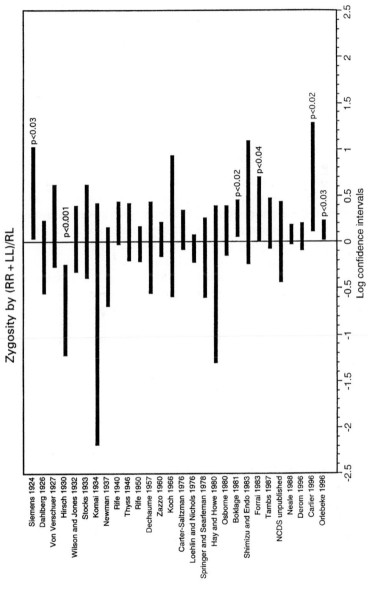

FIG. 4. Log 95% confidence intervals of odds ratios for the 28 studies comparing discordant (RL) and all concordant (RR + LL) twin pairs. Positive values indicate increased concordant pairs (RR + LL) in monozygotic twins.

279

DISCUSSION

This meta-analysis demonstrates that twins are more likely to be left-handed than singletons. It is not surprising that this finding has been disputed in the past, as several of the studies considered individually do not show convincing evidence for an increase in left-handedness among twins. This may be due to sample size, but may also reflect methodological differences among the studies. For example, Ellis and co-workers (Ellis et al., 1988) determined laterality quotients (L.Q.) using the Edinburgh Inventory (Oldfield, 1971), but used a cutoff of 0 to define right-and left-handers, which presumably caused many ambidextrous individuals to be grouped with right-handers. In other studies ambidextrous individuals were classified as left-handed or omitted entirely. Genuine differences between the populations may also exist and may relate to differences in the quality of obstetric and perinatal care. Left-handedness has been shown to be increased among individuals with birth stress or trauma (Bakan, 1971; Williams et al., 1992) although other studies have failed to find this association (Searleman, Porac, and Coren, 1989). Among extremely low birthweight (< 1000 grams at birth) left-handedness occurs more frequently (Saigal, Rosenbaum, Szatmari, & Hoult, 1992), as well as in groups with evidence of neurological impairment including epilepsy, cerebral palsy, autism, and mental retardation (Dellatolas et al., 1993; Gordon, 1921; Lewin, Kohen, & Mathew, 1993). Twins are more likely than singletons to be born prematurely and/or experience perinatal injuries, and it has been suggested that the increase in left-handedness in neurologically intact twins reflects one end of the spectrum of the pathological left-handedness syndrome as formulated by Satz (1972). This explanation suggests that twin populations may include two "types" of left handers; natural and "pathological". If subtle brain injuries related to twin births are the major source of increased left-handedness in twins, improved obstetric care should cause the relative frequency of "pathological" left-handed twins to decrease and the overall incidence of left-handedness to approach that of singletons. Of note is the fact that three of the four studies that fail to show increased left-handedness in twins have been done in the last 10 years.

Although left-handedness is increased overall in twins, monozygotic twins are no more likely to be left-handed than dizygotic twins. This suggests that there is nothing specific about the monozygotic twinning process *per se* that contributes to an excess of left-handedness in twins. This is contrary to predictions made by "mirror imaging" hypotheses that postulate that the monozygotic twinning process uniquely leads to increased left-handedness in monozygotic twins. Exclusion of this possibility makes it possible to explore the issue of twin pair concordance in a more straightforward way.

Having shown that twins are more likely to be left-handed than singletons, but that monozygotic and dizygotic twins do not differ in overall incidence of left-handedness, we can now address the issue of concordance in pairs of twins.

In our large meta-analysis, we have shown that monozygotic twin pairs are more likely to have similar handedness than dizygotic twins, contradicting prior statements, based on smaller sample sizes, that the correlations of handedness in twins did not differ from chance (Laland et al., 1995; Tambs et al., 1987). This finding is difficult to explain by a cultural model of handedness, as monozygotic and dizygotic twins are presumably subjected to very similar parental and societal influences affecting handedness. Recent studies have shown no relationship of handedness with chorionic status (Derom et al., 1996), suggesting that proximity in the womb does not affect handedness concordance. These results provide strong support for the hypothesis that genetic factors play a significant role in the determination of hand preference in humans.

Although the frequent occurrence of monozygotic twins who are discordant for handedness is clearly inconsistent with genetic models that would define right-and left-handedness as dominant or recessive traits, discordance among monozygotic twins does not automatically preclude straightforward inheritance of one or more genes that strongly influence hand preference. Annett (1978) proposed an elegant single allele model of handedness that can account for discordant monozygotic twins. She suggested that humans possess a "right shift" (rs) gene that is dominantly expressed and when present shifts hand preference markedly to the right. When this gene is absent (rs—) the right shift bias is removed, and hand preference becomes a matter of chance, so that on average 50% of rs—individuals are right-handed and 50% are left-handed. This is analogous to the way a gene for situs inversus (iv) in mice operates. In mice who lack the normal gene (iv—) situs inversus develops about 50% of the time, i.e. visceral situs becomes random (Layton, 1976; Supp, Witte, Potter, & Brueckner, 1997). Subsequently, Annett (1985) has modified her theory to account for the increased incidence of left-handedness in twins and males. The concept of inherited randomness is also invoked by McManus's (1985) two-allele genetic model for handedness and cerebral lateralisation. The random determination of the direction of lateralisation in those who lack the genetic bias for the normal direction of asymmetry can readily explain the apparent paradox of genetically identical twins with discordant handedness.

The phenotype of handedness is almost certainly influenced by a variety of factors. Early analyses of handedness in twins focused on discordant handedness in identical twins as a basis for dismissing genetic factors. The potential role of random chance in determining the direction of lateralisation was not understood or considered as a means of explaining discordant handedness until decades later. In the absence of a genetic explanation, those who still favoured biological mechanisms invoked mirror imaging during the process of monozygotic twinning as a developmental explanation for the frequent observation of discordant monozygotic twins. Despite some intriguing embryological observations in which situs inversus was invoked by artificially inducing partial twinning (Nascone & Mercola, 1997; Spemann & Rudd, 1922), this turns out to be the explanation most thoroughly excluded by the twin data, as the overall frequency of left-handedness is not higher in monozygotic than in dizygotic twins. Further evidence refuting the mirror imaging hypothesis is found in two recent studies that show no effect of the presumed timing of the twinning event on handedness (Carlier et al., 1996; Derom et al., 1996). Others have dismissed biological mechanisms entirely, attributing variations in handedness patterns solely to cultural, environmental, or random influences (Laland et al., 1995; Orlebeke et al., 1996; Tambs et al., 1987). To reach such conclusions, it was necessary to either dismiss the twin data on the basis that monozygotic twinning involved unique processes or to find no difference in the frequencies or RR, RL, and LL pairs in monozygotic and dizygotic twins. Neither of these conclusions is supported by our meta-analysis.

Variations in the methods used to determine handedness and zygosity pose problems for interpretation of twin studies. Parental or investigator response bias could lead to higher reported rates of left-handedness in twins, but the majority of the large studies comparing twins versus singletons relied on the objective measure of writing hand to determine handedness. Due to the small number of studies reporting ambidextrous individuals, it was not possible to address the question of whether ambidextrous individuals should be considered as right-handers, left-handers, or a separate group. This is an issue of considerable interest for a variety of studies involving hand preference, and future twin studies of handedness could help to address this issue by reporting quantitative measures of hand preference. Zygosity determinations were frequently made without definitive blood antigen testing. The earliest studies cited might be especially questionable given the notions of twinning that existed earlier in the century. For example, some investigators felt that discordant handedness was a marker of monozygosity. An examination of the individual studies does show more extreme results among the earlier studies, but they are not biased in a particular direction and the group results are driven by the much larger, newer studies. Finally, many investigators have shown the reliability of using questionnaires assessing physical resemblance to accurately determine zygosity (Cederlof, Finberg, Jonsson, & Kaif, 1961; Jablon, Neel, Gershowitz, & Atkinson, 1967; Torgersen, 1979).

Specific inheritance patterns can sometimes be inferred from twin studies by comparing the concordance for a trait in monozygotic twins to that in dizygotic twins. Unfortunately, the assumptions that are made in such analyses are likely to be violated in the twin handedness data by the fact that left-handedness is more common in twins than in singletons. The observed concordance ratios can be reconciled with a wide variety of inheritance patterns once allowances are made for the possibility that some left-handedness is pathological in origin. Non-genetic influences also complicate family studies of the inheritance of handedness, and definitive proof of a particular inheritance pattern may ultimately require identification of the responsible gene(s).

Aside from mirror imaging, we do not interpret our results as excluding any of the many additional non-genetic factors that have been proposed as contributors to the phenotypic expression of handedness. Genetics, randomness, brain injury, cultural biases, sex, and other postnatal and possibly even prenatal environmental factors probably all interact to determine whether a given individual is right-handed or left-handed. Such interactions serve to complicate the relationships between phenotype and genotype, but the twin data on handedness provide strong evidence in favour of genetic mechanisms underlying variations in human hand preference.

Manuscript received 1 July 1997
Revised manuscript received 22 December 1997.

REFERENCES

Annett, M. (1978). *A single gene explanation of right-and left-handedness, and brainedness.* Lancaster, UK: Lancaster Polytechnic Press.

Annett, M. (1985). *Left, right, hand and brain: The right shift theory.* Hove, UK: Lawrence Erlbaum Associates Ltd.

Bakan, P. (1971). Handedness and birth order. *Nature, 229,* 195.

Boklage, C.E. (1981). On the distribution of non-right-handedness among twins and their families. *Acta Geneticae Medicae Gemellologae, 30,* 167–187.

Bouterwek, H. (1938). Rechts–links Abwandlung in Handigkeit and seelischer Artung. *Zeitschrift fuer menschliche Vererbungs-und Konstitutionslehre, 21,* 737–760.

Carlier, M., Spitz, E., Vacher-Lavenu, M.C., Villeger, P., Martin, B., & Michel, F. (1996). Manual performance and laterality in twins of known chorion type. *Behavior Genetics, 26*(4), 409–417.

Carter-Saltzman, L. (1980). Biological and socio-cultural effects on handedness: Comparison between biological and adoptive families. *Science, 209,* 1263–1265.

Carter-Saltzman, L., Scarr-Salapatek, S., Barker, W.B., & Katz, S. (1976). Left-handedness in twins: Incidence and patterns of performance in an adolescent sample. *Behavior Genetics, 6,* 189–203.

Cederlof, R., Friberg, L., Jonsson, E., & Kaif, L. (1961). Studies on similarity diagnosis in twins with the aid of mailed questionnaires. *Acta Genetica et Statistica Medica, 11,* 338–362.

Chamberlain, H.D. (1928). The inheritance of left-handedness. *The Journal of Heredity, 19,* 557–559.

Clark, C.M., Klonoff, H., & Tyhurst, J.S. (1986). Handedness concordance and intelligence discrepancies in identical twins. *Archives of Clinical Neuropsychology, 1,* 351–356.

Collins, R.L. (1970). The sound of one paw clapping: An inquiry into the origins of left handedness. In G. Lindzey & D.D. Thiessen (Eds.), *Contributions to behavior-genetic analysis—The mouse as a prototype* (pp.115–136). New York: Meredith.

Corballis, M.C., & Morgan, M.J. (1978). On the biological basis of human laterality: I. Evidence for a maturational left–right gradient. *The Behavioral and Brain Sciences, 1,* 261–269.

Coren, S. (1992). *The left-hander syndrome: The causes and consequences of left-handedness.* New York: Free Press.

Coren, S. (1994). Twinning is associated with an increased risk of left-handedness and inverted writing hand posture. *Early Human Development, 40,* 23–27.

Dahlberg, G. (1926). *Twin births and twins from a hereditary point of view.* Stockholm: Tidens forlag.

Davis, A., & Annett, M. (1994). Handedness as a function of twinning, age and sex. *Cortex, 30,* 105–111.

Davis, J.O., & Phelps, J.A. (1995). Twins with schizophrenia: Genes or germs? *Schizophrenia Bulletin, 21*(1), 13–18.

Davis, J.O., Phelps, J.A., & Bracha, H.S. (1995). Prenatal development of monozygotic twins and concordance for schizophrenia. *Schizophrenia Bulletin, 21*(3), 357–366.

Dechaume, M.P. (1957). *Contribution a létude de la dominance laterale chez les jumeaux.* Unpublished. [As cited by Zazzo, 1960.]

Dellatolas, G., Luciani, S., Castresana, A., Remy, C., Jallon, P., Laplane, D., & Bancaud, J. (1993). Pathological left-handedness. *Brain, 116,* 1565–1574.

Derom, C., Thiery, E., Vlietinck, R., Loos, R., & Derom, R. (1996). Handedness in twins according to zygosity and chorion type: A preliminary report. *Behavior Genetics, 26*(4), 407–408.

Ellis, S.J., Ellis, P.J., & Marshall, E. (1988). Hand preference in a normal population. *Cortex, 24,* 157–163.

Forrai, G., & Bankovi, G. (1983). A Hungarian twin study on hand clasping, arm folding and tongue curling. *Acta Biologica Hungarica, 34,* 99–106.

Galton, F. (1875) The history of twins, as a criterion of the relative powers of nature and nurture. *Fraser's Magazine, 92,* 566–576.

Gart, J.J. (1970). Point and interval estimation of the common odds ratio in the combination of 2 × 2 tables with fixed marginals. *Biometrika, 57*(3), 471–475.

Geschwind, N., & Galaburda, A.M. (1985). Cerebral lateralization: Biological mechanisms, associations, and pathology: I. A hypothesis and a program for research. *Archives of Neurology, 42*(5), 428–459.

Gilger, J.W., Pennington, B.F., Green, P., Smith, S.M., & Smith, S.D. (1992). Reading disability, immune disorders and non-right-handedness: Twin and family studies of their relations. *Neuropsychologia, 30*(3), 209–227.

Gordon, H. (1921). Left-handedness and mirror writing, especially among defective children. *Brain, 43*(4), 312–368.

Hay, D.A., & Howie, P.M. (1980). Handedness and differences in birthweight of twins. *Perceptual and Motor Skills, 51,* 666.

Hecaen, H., & Ajuriaguerra, J. (1964). *Left-handedness.* New York: Grune & Stratton.

Hecaen, H., De Agostini, M., & Monzon-Montes, A. (1981). Cerebral organization in left-handers. *Brain and Language, 12,* 261–284.

Hicks, R.E., & Kinsbourne, M. (1976). Human handedness: A partial cross-fostering study. *Science, 192,* 908–910.

Hirsch, N.D.M. (1930). *Twins, heredity and environment.* Cambridge, MA: Harvard University Press.

Jablon, S., Neel, J., Gerschowitz, H., & Atkinson, G. (1967). The NAS–NRC twin panel: Methods of construction of the panel, zygosity diagnosis, and proposed use. *American Journal of Human Genetics, 19*(2), 133–161.

James, W. (1983). Twinning, handedness and embryology. *Perceptual and Motor Skills, 56,* 721–721.

Jäncke, L., & Steinmetz, H. (1994). Auditory lateralization in monozygotic twins. *International Journal of Neuroscience, 75,* 57–64.

Koch, H.L. (1966). *Twins and twin relations.* Chicago: University of Chicago Press.

Komai, T., & Fukuoka, G. (1934a). A note on the problem of mirror-imaging in human twins. *Human Biology, 6,* 24–32.

Komai, T., & Fukuoka, G. (1934b). A study on the frequency of left-handedness and left-footedness among Japanese school children. *Human Biology, 6,* 33–42.

Laland, K.N., Kumm, J., Van Horn, J.D., & Feldman, M.W. (1995). A gene-culture model of human handedness. *Behavior Genetics, 25,* 433–445.

Lauterbach, C.E. (1925). Studies in twin resemblances. *Genetics, 10*, 525–568.

Layton, W.M. (1976). Random determination of a developmental process: reversal of normal visceral asymmetry in the mouse. *The Journal of Heredity, 67*, 336–338.

Lewin, J., Kohen, D., & Mathew, G. (1993). Handedness in mental handicap: Investigation into populations of Down's syndrome, epilepsy and autism. *British Journal of Psychiatry, 163*, 674–676.

Liebing, M. (1986). Zur Verteilung der handigkeit bei Vorschulkindern. *Arztliche Jugendkunde, 77*(5), 319–323.

Loehlin, J.C., & Nichols, R.C. (1976). *Heredity, environment and personality: A study of 850 sets of twins.* Austin: University of Texas Press.

Luria, A.R. (1970). *Traumatic aphasia.* The Hague: Mouton.

McManus, I.C. (1980). Handedness in twins: A critical review. *Neuropsychologia, 18*, 347–355.

McManus, I.C. (1985). Handedness, language dominance and aphasia: A genetic model. *Psychological Medicine Monographs Supplement, 8*, 1–140.

McManus, I.C., & Bryden, M.P. (1992). The genetics of handedness, cerebral dominance, and lateralization. In S.J.S. Isabelle Rapin (Ed.), *Handbook of neuropsychology* (pp.115–144). Amsterdam, Netherlands: Elsevier Science Publishing Co, Inc.

Mehta, C.R. (1994). The exact analysis of contingency tables in medical research. *Statistical Methods in Medical Research, 3*, 135–56.

Morley, R., & Caffrey, E.A. (1994). Handedness in blood donors: No association with blood group or twinning. *Cortex, 30*, 707–710.

Nagylaki, T., & Levy, J. (1973). ''The sound of one paw clapping' isn't sound. *Behavior Genetics, 3*, 279–292.

Nascone, N., & Mercola, M. (1997). Organizer induction determines left–right asymmetry in Xenopus. *Developmental Biology, 189*(1), 68–78.

Neale, M.C. (1988). Handedness in a sample of volunteer twins. *Behavior Genetics, 18*, 69–79.

Newman, H.H. (1928). Studies of human twins: II. Asymmetry reversal, of mirror imaging in identical twins. *Biological Bulletin, 55*, 298–315.

Newman, H.H., Freeman, F.N., & Holzinger, K.J. (1937). *Twins, a study of heredity and environment.* Chicago: University of Chicago Press.

Oldfield, R.C. (1971). The assessment and analysis of handedness: The Edinburgh inventory. *Neuropsychologia, 9*, 97–113.

Orlebeke, J.F., Knol, D.L., Koopmans, J.R., Boomsma, D.I., & Bleker, O.P. (1996). Left-handedness in twins: Genes or environment? *Cortex, 32*, 479–490.

Osborne, R.T. (1980). *Twins: Black and White.* Athens: Foundation for Human Understanding.

Perelle, I., & Ehrman, L. (1994). An international study of human handedness: The data. *Behavior Genetics, 24*(3), 217–227.

Rife, D.C. (1940). Handedness, with special reference to twins. *Genetics, 25*, 178–186.

Rife, D.C. (1950). An application of gene frequency analysis to the interpretation of data from twins. *Human Biology, 22*, 136–145.

Saigal, S., Rosenbaum, P.L., Szatmari, P., & Hoult, L. (1992). Non-right handedness among ELBW and term children at eight years in relation to cognitive function and school performance. *Developmental Medicine & Child Neurology, 34*(5), 425–433.

Satz, P. (1972). Pathological left-handedness: An explanatory model. *Cortex, 8*, 121–135.

Satz, P., Orsini, D.L., Saslow, E., & Henry, R. (1985). The pathological left-handedness syndrome. *Brain and Cognition, 4*, 27–46.

Searleman, A., Porac, C., & Coren, S. (1989). Relationship between birth order, birth stress, and lateral preferences: A critical review. *Psychological Bulletin, 105*(3), 397–408.

Segal, N.L. (1989). Origins and implications of handedness and relative birth weight for I.Q. in monozygotic pairs. *Neuropsychologia, 27*(4), 549–561.

Shields, J. (1962). *Monozygotic twins: Brought up apart and brought up together.* London: Oxford University Press.

Shimizu, A., & Endo, M. (1983). Comparison of patterns of handedness between twins and singletons in Japan. *Cortex, 19*, 345–352.

Siemens, H.W. (1924). Uber Linkshandigkeit. *Virchow's Archives, 252*, 1–24.

Spemann, H., & Rudd, G. (1922). Situs inversus, asymmetry and twinning. *American Journal of Human Genetics, 2*, 361–370.

Springer, S.P., & Searleman, A. (1978). Laterality in twins: The relationship between handedness and hemispheric asymmetry for speech. *Behavior Genetics, 8*, 349–357.

Springer, S.P., & Searleman, A. (1978). The ontogeny of hemispheric specialization: Evidence from dichotic listening in twins. *Neuropsychologia, 16*, 269–281.

Stocks, P. (1933). A biometric investigation of twins and their brothers and sisters. *Annals of Eugenics, 5*, 1–55.

Subirana, A. (1958). The prognosis in aphasia in relation to cerebral dominance and handedness. *Brain, 81*, 415–425.

Supp, D.M., Witte, D.P., Potter, S.S., & Brueckner, M. (1997). Mutation of an axonemal dynein affects left–right asymmetry in inversus viscerum mice. *Nature, 389*, 963.

Tambs, K., Magnus, P., & Berg, K. (1987). Left-handedness in twin families: Support of an environmental hypothesis. *Perceptual and Motor Skills, 64*, 155–170.

Teng, E.L., Lee, P., Yang, K., & Chang, P.C. (1976). Handedness in a Chinese population: Biological, social and pathological factors. *Science, 193*, 1148–1150.

Thyss, J. (1946). *Etude bibliographique et critique du problème des gauchers.* Unpublished. [As cited by Zazzo, 1960.]

Torgersen, S. (1979). The determination of zygosity by means of a mailed questionnaire. *Acta Geneticae Medicae Gemellologae, 28*, 225–236.

von Verschuer, O. (1927). Die vererbungsbiologische zwillingsforschung. *Ergebnisse der Inneren Medizin und Kinderheilkunde, 31*, 35–102.

Weitz, W. (1924). Studien an eineiigen Zwillingen. *Zeitschrift für Klinische Medizin, 101*, 115–154.

Williams, C.S., Buss, K.A., & Eskenazi, B. (1992). Infant resuscitation is associated with an increased risk of left-handedness. *American Journal of Epidemiology, 136*, 277–286.

Wilson, P.T., & Jones, H.E. (1932). Left-handedness in twins. *Genetics, 17*, 560–571.

Zazzo, R. (1960). *Les jumeaux: Le couple et la personne.* Paris: Presses Universitaires de France.

LATERALITY, 1999, 4 (3), 287–297

Laterality of Hand, Foot, Eye, and Ear in Twins

Michael Reiss, Gerd Tymnik, Petra Kögler, Wolfgang Kögler, and Gilfe Reiss

University of Dresden, Germany

Information on handedness, footedness, eyedness, and earedness was collected from 33 monozygotic (MZ) twin pairs and 67 dizygotic (DZ) twin pairs. The incidence of nonright-sidedness in the twins is not higher than that reported in the literature for singletons. Similar results are found for the other lateralities. The results of assessing handedness with preference tests do not differ from those carried out with performance tests. There are no differences in incidence of nonright-sidedness between MZ and DZ twins. The concordance of lateralities is similar in MZ and DZ twins. The proportions of Right–Right, Right–Nonright, and Nonright–Nonright pairs in both groups of twins show a binomial distribution. The present results do not confirm a genetic hypothesis of determination of sidedness in humans and are comparable with the results obtained by other twin studies.

INTRODUCTION

The relationship between handedness and cerebral lateralisation is of interest because the two hemispheres of the brain perform different functions (Annett, 1985; Bradshaw, 1989; Bryden, 1982; Corballis, 1991; Morgan, 1991). Most humans show a preference for using one hand rather than the other for a wide variety of manual tasks (Coren, 1994c; McManus, 1984; Peters, 1991). Handedness can be assessed either as preference or skill. Hand preference is commonly established using a questionnaire. However, for the study of a young population it is preferable to observe the child performing activities such as writing or throwing a ball (Coren, 1994c; Coren, Porac, & Duncan, 1981; McManus, 1984; Strauss & Goldsmith, 1987). It is also important to distinguish between direction of preference (being right- or left-handed) and degree of preference (being strongly or weakly handed).

Requests for reprints should be sent to M. Reiss, MD, Department of Ear, Nose and Throat, University of Dresden, Fetscherstr. 74, D-01307 Dresden, Germany.

Gerd Tymnik was formerly at the Department of Ear, Nose and Throat, University of Dresden; present address: D-01558 Großenhain, Meißner Landstr. 84. Petra Kögler and Wolfgang Kögler were formerly doctorands at the Department of Ear, Nose and Throat, University of Dresden. Gilfe Reiss is at the Department of Neurosurgery, University of Dresden.

It is still a matter of dispute whether handedness is determined primarily by genetic or non-genetic factors. There is considerable evidence for familial aggregation of handedness (Annett, 1996; Bryden, 1989; Coren, 1994a; McManus, 1985, 1991). A number of genetic models have been proposed to account for the family data, but one of the classic methods for testing hypotheses—the twin method—has consistently yielded data that at first sign seem incompatible with a genetic component. However, the twin method is often midunderstood. The critical analysis compares monozygotic (MZ) twins, who have identical genes, with (dizygotic) DZ twins, who share only half their genes. An increased concordance of MZ compared with DZ twins may then be attributed to genetic factors. The literature shows that there is indeed a slightly higher rate of concordance in MZ twins than in DZ twins (McManus, 1980; Reiss, 1996; Springer & Searleman, 1980).

Previous studies of lateralisation in twins have focused mainly on handedness. Here we report, for the first time, studies of footedness (foot preference), eyedness (eye preference), and earedness (ear preference) in twins.

METHOD

Subjects

The study group was made up of 33 MZ and 67 DZ pairs, all aged between 10 and 25 years (mean 15.5, SD = 3.4). All twins were born in Dresden or the nearby town of Görlitz.

Zygosity was determined by serological analysis, incorporating 16 immuno-genetic tests (Department of Forensic Science, University of Leipzig).

Procedure

Each twin was individually tested three times on the behavioural measures of laterality preference.

Hand preference was assessed with a test battery including 12 tasks: using a hammer, playing at dice, nose–forefinger-test, drawing, writing, cleaning teeth, setting an alarm-clock, opening a bottle, moving a ring on a pole, serving a ball, combing hair, and opening and shutting a zipper.

Hand preference was assessed using a modified paper-and-pencil perfor-mance test described by Steingrüber and Lienert (1976) comprising a dexterity task to be performed with maximal speed and precision (dotting circles). Performance was scored three times for each hand. Hand dominance was calculated using the following index.

$$\text{Dominance} = \frac{(\text{right-hand performance}) - (\text{left-hand performance})}{(\text{right-hand performance}) + (\text{left-hand performance})} \times 100$$

This formula gives a continuous score for hand dominance ranging from –100, consistent left to +100, consistent right. We classified any individual achieving score from –100 to < 0 as nonright-handed, while those with scores ranging from 0 to +100 were classified as right-handed.

Footedness (foot preference) was assessed with five tasks: hopping, kicking a ball (sitting), kicking a ball (standing), drawing a figure with the foot (sitting), and drawing a figure with the foot (standing).

Eyedness (eye preference). There was one question: "Which eye do you use when peeping through a key hole?"

Earedness (ear preference). The twin was required to listen to a clock in a box.

Left-preference in a task was scored as one point, right-preference as zero, and no preference as a half point (Oeser, 1973). This procedure established a continuous score for hand preference ranging from 12, consistent left, to 0, consistent right. We classified any individual achieving a score from 12 to > 6 as nonright-handed, while those scores ranging from 0 to 6 were called right-handed. For foot preference the scores ranged from 5, consistent left, to 0, consistent right. Individuals achieving a score from 5 to > 2.5 are nonright-footed and from 0 to 2.5 are right-footed. In the case of eyedness and earedness scores ranged from 1, left-sided, to 0, right-sided. We classified any individual achieving a score from 1.0 to > 0.5 as nonright-sided, while those scores ranging from 0 to 0.5 were called right-sided.

RESULTS

Distribution

The frequencies of nonright-sidedness of hand preference, hand performance, footedness, eyedness, and earedness in twins' samples are shown in Table 1. None of the five measures showed significant differences between MZ and DZ twins.

Interrelationship

Table 2 gives the correlation between the various lateralities (hand preference/ hand dominance, hand preference/foot preference, hand preference/eye preference, and so on) for all twins, and for MZ-and DZ-twins separately. Three of the ten possible combinations are statistically significant: hand dominance/hand preference, foot preference/hand preference, and hand dominance/foot preference. Table 2 shows no difference between MZ- and DZ-twins. Five of the ten combinations show a higher correlation in MZ than in DZ-twins.

TABLE 1
Right- and Nonright-sidedness in 66 MZ and 123 DZ Twins

		MZ Twins	DZ Twins	MZ and DZ Twins	χ^2-Test DF = 1	Significance
Hand	Right	61 (.924)	125 (.933)	186 (.93)	.050	NS
Preference	Nonright	5 (.076)	9 (.067)	14 (.07)		
Hand	Right	61 (.924)	119 (.888)	180 (.9)	.643	NS
Dominance	Nonright	5 (.076)	15 (.112)	20 (.1)		
Foot	Right	62 (.940)	120 (.895)	182 (.91)	1.039	NS
Preference	Nonright	4 (.060)	14 (.105)	18 (.09)		
Eye Preference	Right	42 (.636)	73 (.545)	115 (.575)	1.1518	NS
	Nonright	24 (.364)	61 (.455)	85 (.425)		
Ear Preference	Right	44 (.667)	91 (.679)	135 (.675)	.031	NS
	Nonright	22 (.333)	43 (.321)	65 (.325)		

Combinations Within Twin-pairs

The pairwise combinations of hand preference, hand dominance, footedness, eyedness, and earedness are shown in Table 3. The three possible combinations (Right–Right, Right–Nonright, Nonright–Nonright) do not significantly differ between MZ and DZ twins for any of the lateralities.

Table 4 compares the distribution of laterality measures within twin pairs with a binomial distribution: none shows any significant differences from binomiality.

DISCUSSION

To our knowledge this is the first study in literature assessing simultaneously four lateralities in MZ and DZ twins: handedness, footedness, eyedness, and earedness (compare Kovác & Ruisel, 1974). There are many studies that examine handedness in twins. Reiss (1996) identified 40 studies and another 4 have recently been published (Carlier et al., 1996; Derom et al., 1996; Jäncke & Steinmetz, 1995; Orlebeke et al., 1996). Concerning the other lateralities there are only a few studies: foot preference (Kovác & Ruisel, 1974; von Verschuer, 1927), eye preference (Kovác & Ruisel, 1974; Rife, 1933), visual acuity dominance (Stocks, 1933), ear preference (Kovác & Ruisel, 1974), dichotic listening (Springer & Searleman, 1978), auditory acuity dominance (Steinert, 1968), EEG asymmetry (Meshkova, 1992; Raney, 1939), hand clasping (Dahlberg, 1926; Forrai & Bankovi, 1983; Martin, 1975; von Verschuer, 1932), and arm folding (Forrai & Bankovi, 1983; von Verschuer, 1932). Several authors investigated laterality only in MZ twins. Kovác and Ruisel (1974) examined the preference of hand, foot, eye, and ear in only 11 MZ twin pairs. Jäncke &

TABLE 2

Correlations Among Measures of Laterality for all Twins and for MZ and DZ Separately

	Hand Preference	Hand Dominance	Foot Preference	Eye Preference	Ear Preference
Hand Preference	1.000	Total: .682 (<.0001) MZ: .657 (<.0001) DZ: .700 (<.0001)	Total: .515 (<.0001) MZ: .550 (<.0001) DZ: .501 (<.0001)	Total: .126 (.0541) MZ: .230 (.0636) DZ: .090 (.3001)	Total: .212 (.0025) MZ: .120 (.3400) DZ: .262 (.0022)
Hand Dominance		1.000	Total: .440 (<.0001) MZ: .436 (.0002) DZ: .441 (<.0001)	Total: .035 (.6253) MZ: .167 (.1820) DZ: −.021 (.8115)	Total: .200 (.0044) MZ: .176 (.1591) DZ: .216 (.0121)
Foot Preference			1.000	Total: .172 (.0145) MZ: .238 (.0537) DZ: .139 (.1081)	Total: .085 (.2334) MZ: −.171 (.1715) DZ: .207 (.0161)
Eye Preference				1.000	Total: .138 (.0517) MZ: .154 (.2171) DZ: .134 (.1229)
Ear Preference					1.000

P-values (Fisher's transformation) in parentheses.

291

TABLE 3
Concordance of the Five Lateralities in MZ and DZ Twins

Combination	Hand Preference		Hand Performance		Foot Preference		Eye Preference		Ear Preference	
	MZ Twins	DZ Twins	MZ Twins	DZ Twins	MZ Twins	DZ Twins	MZ Twins	DZ Twins	MZ Twins	DZ Twins
Right–Right	28 (.848)	58 (.866)	28 (.848)	55 (.797)	29 (.879)	54 (.806)	16 (.485)	26 (.388)	12 (.364)	31 (.463)
Right–Nonright	5 (.152)	9 (.134)	5 (.152)	9 (.134)	4 (.121)	12 (.179)	10 (.303)	21 (.313)	20 (.606)	29 (.433)
Nonright–Nonright	0	0	0	3 (.045)	0	1 (.015)	7 (.212)	20 (.299)	1 (.030)	7 (.104)
Concordance	.848	.866	.848	.842	.879	.821	.697	.687	.394	.567
χ^2-Test (DF = 1)	.080		.080		.842		.017		3.563	
Significance	NS		NS		NS		NS		NS	

Proportions in brackets.

TABLE 4
Analysis of Goodness of Fit of a Binomial Distribution for the Five Laterality Measures

	Hand Preference	Hand Dominance	Foot Preference	Eye Preference	Ear Preference
N MZ-pairs	33	33	33	33	33
Theoretical values					
Right–Right	29.028	29.028	29.979	13.753	15.126
Right–Nonright	4.775	4.775	3.895	15.742	15.104
Nonright–Nonright	.196	.196	.127	4.505	3.770
Difference to Binomial distribution					
Right–Right (relative)	−.005	−.005	−.003	.080	−.081
Right–Nonright (relative)	.011	.011	.007	−.160	.162
Nonright–Nonright (rel.)	−.006	−.006	−.004	.080	−.081
χ^2 (DF = 2)	.001	.001	.0002	.837	2.833
Significance	NS	NS	NS	NS	NS
N DZ-pairs	67	67	67	67	67
Theoretical values					
Right–Right	57.452	52.044	52.868	19.604	30.071
Right–Nonright	8.251	13.128	12.405	32.733	28.958
Nonright–Nonright	.296	.828	.728	13.664	6.971
Difference to Binomial distribution					
Right–Right (relative)	−.005	.009	.005	.091	.007
Right–Nonright (relative)	.009	−.039	−.009	−.183	−.006
Nonright–Nonright (rel.)	−.004	.031	.004	.091	−.001
χ^2 (DF = 2)	.036	1.185	.002	3.501	.009
Significance	NS	NS	NS	NS	NS

Steinmetz, 1995), dichotic listening (Jäncke & Steinmetz, 1994), and also brain asymmetry (Steinmetz et al., 1995) only in MZ twins. Unfortunately studies of only MZ twins allow no further analysis. The statement by Jäncke and Steinmetz (1995), based only on the study of MZ twins, that laterality is mainly determined by non-genetic factors, is therefore not correct.

In the literature there are several suggestions that the incidence of left-handedness or nonright-handedness is higher in twins than in singletons, and that MZ twins are more likely to be left-handed than DZ twins (Collins, 1970; Nagylaki & Levy, 1973). In the present study the incidence of nonright-handedness is not significantly higher than in other populations reported in the literature (Bourassa, McManus, & Bryden, 1996; Ellis, Ellis, & Marshall, 1988; Porac & Coren, 1981). There are also no differences between MZ and DZ twins. The relatively low incidence of nonright-handedness must also be seen in the light of our relative broad criterion of nonright-handedness comparing a laterality quotient <0 and in the relative young age of the twins. There are reports in the literature that left-handedness decreases with age (Brown, McCarthy, & Wolpert, 1990; Coren & Hakstian, 1992; Longoni & Orsini, 1988; Porac, 1993). The incidence of nonright-sidedness for footedness, eyedness, and earedness in twins is not noticeably higher in our study than the incidence in singletons (Bourassa et al., 1996; Corballis, 1983; Hoogmartens & Caubergh, 1987; Mandal, Pandey, Singh, & Asthana, 1992; Porac & Coren, 1981) and there are no significant differences between MZ and DZ twins. The correlation between lateralities conforms with that reported in the literature for singletons (e.g. Bourassa et al., 1996; Longoni & Orsini, 1988).

It has been claimed that the distribution of MZ and DZ handedness pairs approximates to a binomial distribution (Collins, 1970), and our data show the same effect for all five laterality measures.

In summary, the present findings indicate that the incidence of nonright-handedness in twins is not higher than that reported in the literature for singletons. The results of assessing handedness with preference tests do not differ from those carried out with performance tests. The incidence of nonright-sidedness for foot, eye, or ear is also not obviously higher than in singletons. There are no differences in incidence and concordance between MZ and DZ twins for any of the lateralities. The present results do not confirm a genetic hypothesis of determination of sidedness in humans. Taking the literature as a whole, there are factors favouring a genetic influence (presence of asymmetries in infants and their correlation with cerebral dominance, structural and behavioural asymmetries, certainly highly heritable traits) and also those compatible with sociocultural determination (twin data) (Annett, 1985; Bradshaw, 1989; Bryden, 1982; Corballis, 1991; Morgan, 1991). Family studies on handedness, however, show a clear intrafamiliar relationship. Data from adoption studies on handedness are rare but they suggest that the effects of shared biological heritage are more powerful determinants of handedness than sociocultural factors (Annett, 1996; Bryden, 1989; Coren, 1994a; McManus, 1985, 1991). Although the twin data may in isolation be seen as rejecting an influence of genes on lateralisation, it must be emphasised that genetic models incorporating a chance factor predict only a very low concordance of twins, a similar order to that which is indeed found (McManus, 1991).

Manuscript received 17 March 1997
Revised manuscript received 1 September 1998

REFERENCES

Annett, M. (1985). *Left, right, hand and brain: The right shift theory.* Hove, UK: Lawrence Erlbaum.

Annett, M. (1996). In defence of the right shift theory. *Perceptual and Motor Skills, 82*, 115–37.

Bourassa, D.C., McManus, I.C., & Bryden, M.P. (1996). Handedness and eye-dominance: A meta-analysis of their relationship. *Laterality, 1*, 5–34.

Bradshaw, J.L. (1989). *Hemispheric specialization and psychological function.* Chichester & New York: John Wiley.

Brown, N.A., McCarthy, A., & Wolpert, L. (1990). The development of handed asymmetry in aggregation chimeras of situs inversus mutans and wild-type mouse embryo. *Development, 110*, 949–954.

Bryden, M.P. (1982). *Laterality: Functional asymmetry in the intact brain.* New York: Academic Press.

Bryden, M.P. (1989). Handedness, cerebral lateralization, and measures of ''latent left-handedness''. *International Journal of Neuroscience, 44*, 227–233.

Carlier, M., Spitz, E., Vacher Lavenu, M.C., Villeger, P., Martin, B., & Michel, F. (1996). Manual performance and laterality in twins of known chorion type. *Behavior Genetics, 26*, 409–407.

Collins, R.L. (1970). The sound of one paw clapping: An inquiry into the origin of left-handedness. In G. Lindzey & D. Thiessen (Eds.), *Contributions to behavior-genetic analysis: The mouse as a prototype* (pp.115–135). New York: Appleton Century Crofts.

Corballis, M.C. (1983). *Human laterality.* New York: Academic Press.

Corballis, M.C. (1991). *The lop-sided ape: Evolution of the generative mind.* New York: Oxford University Press.

Coren, S. (1994a). Are fingerprints a genetic marker for handedness? *Behavior Genetics, 24*, 141–148.

Coren, S. (1994b). Methodological problems in determining the relationship between handedness and immune system function. *Brain and Cognition, 26*, 168–173.

Coren, S. (1994c). The prevalence of self-reported sleep disturbances in young adults. *International Journal of Neuroscience, 79*, 67–73.

Coren, S., & Hakstian, A.R. (1992). The development and cross-validation of a self-report inventory to assess pure-tone threshold hearing sensitivity. *Journal of Speech and Hearing Research, 35*, 921–928.

Coren, S., Porac, C., & Duncan, P. (1981). Lateral preference behaviors in preschool children and young adults. *Child Development, 52*, 443–450.

Dahlberg, G. (1926). *Twin births and twins from a hereditary point of view.* Thesis, University of Stockholm.

Derom, C., Thiery, E., Vlietinck, R., Loos, R., & Derom, R. (1996). Handedness in twins according to zygosity and chorion type: A preliminary report. *Behavior Genetics, 26*, 407–408.

Ellis, S.J., Ellis, P.J., & Marshall, E. (1988). Hand preference in a normal population. *Cortex, 24*, 157–163.

Forrai, G., & Bankovi, G. (1983). A Hungarian twin study on hand clasping, arm folding and tongue curling. *Acta Biologica Hungaria, 34*, 99–106.

Hoogmartens, M.J., & Caubergh, M.A.A. (1987). Chewing side preference during the first chewing cycle. *Electromyography and Clinical Neurophysiology, 27*, 3–6.

Jäncke, L., & Steinmetz, H. (1994). Auditory lateralization in monozygotic twins. *International Journal of Neuroscience, 75*, 57–74.

Jäncke, L., & Steinmetz, H. (1995). Hand motor performance and degree of asymmetry in monozygotic twins. *Cortex, 31*, 779–785.

Kovác, D., & Ruisel, I. (1974). Are monozygotic twins identical as regards lateral preferences? *Studia Psychologia, 16*, 217–219.

Longoni, A.M., & Orsini, L. (1988). Lateral preferences in preschool children: A research note. *Journal of Child Psychology & Psychiatry & Allied Disciplines, 29*, 533–539.

Mandal, M.K., Pandey, G., Singh, S.K., & Asthana, H.S. (1992). Degree of asymmetry in lateral preferences: Eye, foot, ear. *Journal of Psychology, 126*, 155–162.

Martin, N.G. (1975). No evidence for a genetic basis of tongue rolling or hand clasping. *Journal of Heredity, 66*, 179–180.

McManus, I.C. (1980). Handedness in twins: A critical review. *Neuropsychologia, 18*, 347–355.

McManus, I.C. (1984). Genetics of handedness in relation to language disorder. *Advances in Neurology, 42*, 125–38.

McManus, I.C. (1985). Handedness, language dominance and aphasia: A genetic model. *Psychological Medicine Supplement, 8*, 1–40.

McManus, I.C. (1991). The inheritance of left-handedness. *Ciba Foundation Symposium, 162*, 251–267.

Meshkova, T.A. (1992). Laterality effects in twins. *Acta Genetica Medica et Gemellologica Roma, 41*, 325–333.

Morgan, M.J. (1991). The asymmetrical genetic determination of laterality: Flatfish, frogs and human handedness. *Ciba Foundation Symposium, 162*, 234–247.

Nagylaki, T., & Levy, J. (1973). "The sound of one paw clapping" is not sound. *Behavior Genetics, 3*, 279–292.

Oeser, R. (1973). Händigkeitsstufen, Lebensalter und Geschlecht: Untersuchungen an 7- bis 17-jährigen Probanden. *Ärztliche Jugendkunde, 64*, 437–447.

Orlebeke, J.F., Knol, D.L., Koopmans, J.R., Boomsma, D.I., & Bleker, O.P. (1996). Left-handedness in twins: Genes or environment? *Cortex, 32*, 479–490.

Peters, M. (1991). Laterality and motor control. *Ciba Foundation Symposium, 162*, 300–301.

Porac, C. (1993). Are age trends in adult hand preference best explained by developmental shifts or generational differences? *Canadian Journal of Experimental Psychology, 47*, 697–713.

Porac, C., & Coren, S. (1981). *Lateral preferences and human behavior.* New York, Heidelberg, Berlin: Springer Verlag.

Raney, E.T. (1939). Brain potentials and lateral dominance in identical twins. *Journal of Experimental Psychology, 24*, 21–39.

Reiss, M. (1996). Zur Lateralität bei Zwillingen. *Zeitschrift für Morphologie und Anthropologie, 81*, 141–155.

Rife, D.C. (1933). Genetic studies of monozygotic twins. III Mirror imaging. *Journal of Heredity, 24*, 443–446.

Springer, S.P., & Searleman, A. (1978). Laterality in twins: The relation between handedness and hemispheric asymmetry for speech. *Behavior Genetics, 8*, 349–357.

Springer, S.P., & Searleman, A. (1980). Left-handedness in twins: Implications for the mechanisms underlying cerebral asymmetry of function. In J. Herron (Ed.). *Neuropsychology of left-handedness* (pp.139–158). New York: Academic Press.

Steinert, R. (1968). *Phoniatrische und audiologische Untersuchungen bei ein- und zweieiigen Zwillingen.* Unpublished Thesis, University of Dresden.

Steingrüber, H.-J., & Lienert, G.A. (1976). *Hand-Dominanz-Test* (2nd Edn.). Göttingen: Hogrefe.

Steinmetz, H., Herzog, A., Schlaug, G., Huang, Y., & Jäncke, L. (1995). Brain (A)symmetry in monozygotic twins. *Cerebral Cortex, 5,* 296–300.

Stocks, P. (1933). A biometrical investigation of twins and their brothers and sisters. *Annals of Eugenics, 5,* 1–55.

Strauss, E., & Goldsmith, S.M. (1987). Lateral preferences and performance on non-verbal laterality tests in a normal population. *Cortex, 23,* 495–503.

von Verschuer, O. (1927). Die vererbungsbiologische Zwillingsforschung. Ihre biologischen Grundlagen. Studien an 102 eineiigen und 45 gleichgeschlechtlichen zweieiigen Zwillings- und Drillingspaaren. *Ergebnisse der inneren Medizin und Kinderheilkunde, 31,* 35–120.

von Verschuer, O. (1932). Die biologischen Grundlagen der menschlichen Mehrlingsforschung. *Induktive Abstammungs-und Vererbungslehre, 61,* 145–207.

LATERALITY, 1999, *4* (3), 299–311

A Twin Study of Individual Differences in Perceptual Asymmetry

Eve M. Valera, Wendy Heller, and Howard Berenbaum

University of Illinois at Urbana-Champaign, USA

Individual differences in perceptual asymmetry have been associated with individual differences in cognitive abilities, personality characteristics, and psychiatric symptoms, for which between-person variation appears to be genetically influenced. Perceptual asymmetry scores are also associated with direction of handedness, for which between-person variation does not appear to be genetically influenced. To assess whether between-person variation of perceptual asymmetry scores is genetically influenced, we examined asymmetry on a free-vision task of face processing, the Chimeric Faces Task (CFT), in a sample of 31 monozygotic (MZ) and 20 same-sex dizygotic (DZ) twin pairs. MZ and DZ within-twin-pair resemblances were compared to assess genetic and familial influences on asymmetric hemispheric function. We found that twins within a pair were no more likely to resemble each other than were unrelated individuals. The results suggest that the between-person variation in CFT perceptual asymmetry is not influenced by genes or shared environment.

INTRODUCTION

Performance differences for specific types of information have been observed when visual, auditory, and tactile stimuli are presented to lateralised sensory channels. These perceptual asymmetries have been related to hemispheric specialisation (for review, see Heller, 1991). Left hemisphere specialisation for linguistic information processing leads to superior performance on syllable, word, and other language stimuli when they are presented to the contralateral (right) visual field, ear, or body side. Conversely, right hemisphere specialisation for spatial and emotional information leads to superior performance for stimuli in these categories when they are presented to the left field, ear, or side.

Requests for reprints should be sent to Eve M. Valera, Department of Psychology, University of Illinois, Urbana-Champaign, 603 E. Daniel Street. Champaign, IL 61820, USA.

The authors would like to thank the National Organization of Mothers of Twins Clubs for their assistance in recruiting twins for this study.

Perceptual asymmetries emerge under conditions when information is initially restricted to one hemisphere, such as in tachistoscopic presentation (Bradshaw & Nettleton, 1983). They have also been shown to be a robust phenomenon under free-viewing conditions when information is readily available to both hemispheres (Heller, 1991). Hemispatial biases have emerged for verbal material, with better performance in the right half of space (Levy & Kueck, 1985; Tressoldi, 1987), and for nonverbal material (Tressoldi, 1987), with better performance in the left half of space.

A highly reliable and robust hemispatial bias is also shown by right-handed people for happiness judgements on the Chimeric Faces Task (CFT; Levy, Heller, Banich, & Burton, 1983a,b). Split-faces with smiles appearing in the left half of space are perceived as happier than faces with smiles in the right half of space. Similar biases favouring the left side of space have been shown for judgement of happiness for cartoon chimeras, for judgement of femininity for male/female chimeras, and for judgement of shape on spatial chimeras (Luh, Rueckert, & Levy, 1991).These hemispatial biases have been interpreted to reflect an increase in the salience of left-sided information, presumably associated with an orienting response produced by increased activity of the contralateral (right) hemisphere (Levy et al., 1983a). As expected for a task that engages specialised hemispheric processes, left-and right-handers differ in the magnitude and variance of hemispatial biases. Left-handers typically show a reduced or absent hemispatial bias, and the variance in their scores is larger (Hellige et al., 1994; Kim, 1994).

Although hemispatial biases are produced by hemispheric specialisation for specific types of information, there are large individual differences in the magnitude and direction of these asymmetries. On the CFT, these individual differences have been shown to be consistent for different stimulus items (.93 split-half reliability) and stable over time (.87 test–retest reliability; Levy et al., 1983b). Furthermore, hemispatial bias is correlated with individual differences in direction and magnitude of perceptual asymmetry on tachistoscopic tasks (Kim & Levine, 1991, 1992; Kim, Levine, & Kertesz, 1990; Levy et al., 1983b; Wirsen, Klinteberg, Levander, & Schalling, 1990), which in turn have been shown to be associated with stable asymmetries in EEG alpha activity (Green et al., 1992).

A number of studies have examined the factors contributing to variation in CFT scores. Approximately 50% is accounted for by trait-like, task-independent characteristic biases. Another 27% may be accounted for by the cumulative effects of a number of task-dependent lateralised or hemisphere-specialised processes (i.e. facial or emotional processes; Hoptman & Levy, 1988). In summary, perceptual asymmetry scores reflect both hemispheric specialisation and characteristics biases (Kim & Levine, 1991).

Patterns of perceptual asymmetry are associated with several aspects of human functioning. They have been shown to be associated with individual differences in cognitive functions (Banich, Elledge, & Stolar, 1992; Levy et al., 1983a), and personality characteristics such as alexithymia (Berenbaum & Prince, 1994), extraversion (Berenbaum & Williams, 1994; Charman, 1979), and pessimism (Levy et al., 1983a). Patterns of perceptual asymmetry have also been associated with symptoms of anxiety and depression (e.g. Heller, Etienne, & Miller, 1995), as well as with a variety of psychiatric disturbances such as major depressive disorder, bipolar disorder, dysthymia, and schizophrenia (for review, see Bruder, 1995). Research has consistently demonstrated that the between-person variation of such personality characteristics/psychopathology is genetically influenced (e.g. Carey & DiLalla, 1994; for review, see McCartney, Harris, & Bernierni, 1990).

As mentioned earlier, perceptual asymmetry scores are also associated with direction of handedness. However, unlike other phenomena associated with patterns of perceptual asymmetry, research has generally found that dizygotic (DZ) twins are just as likely to be concordant for handedness as are monozygotic (MZ) twins, and whether they are MZ or DZ, twins are no more likely to have the same handedness than are two random individuals (e.g. Corballis & Beale, 1976; Coren, 1992; Derom et al., 1996; Laland, Kumm, Van Horn, & Feldman, 1995; Orlebeke et al, 1996).[1] This evidence suggests that genes account for very little, if any, of the between-person variation in handedness. Several researchers (e.g. Annett, 1978, 1985, 1996; McManus, 1985) have proposed complex diallelic models of handedness. These models propose that genes do influence handedness, but that "almost all of the variability between twins is random" (Annett, 1996, p.119). Annett (1996, p.119) further states that "the greater concordance of genotypes in MZ pairs in comparison with DZ pairs has so small an effect on handedness, in comparison with the random variance, that enormous samples are necessary to demonstrate the effect." Thus, according to these models, genes may explain why most humans are right-handed; however, the available twin and family data suggest that genes do not account for much of the between-person variation in handedness (Annett, 1996).

These research findings led us to examine whether between-person variation of CFT asymmetry scores would be genetically influenced as is the case with psychopathology/personality, or would not be genetically influenced as appears to be the case with handedness. In this study, we used the CFT to assess perceptual asymmetry and compared MZ and DZ within-twin-pair resemblances. To the extent that MZ twin pairs are more similar in their CFT scores than are DZ twin pairs, a genetic component can be inferred.

---

[1] Carlier et al. (1996) examined co-twin resemblance of manual performance in MZ and DZ twins. Similar to results of the handedness literature, the results of Carlier et al. indicate that between-person variation of manual performance does not appear to be genetically influenced.

METHOD

Participants

Participants were 64 twin pairs recruited through newspaper advertisements, sign-up sheets in a midwestern university campus and community, and through the aid of the National Organization of Mothers of Twins Club. After twins were screened for handedness and assessed for zygosity, a total of 51 pairs were eligible for CFT data analyses. Ten pairs of twins were eliminated from CFT analyses because at least one twin was left-handed, and three pairs were eliminated because zygosity could not be unanimously determined. Only same-sex DZ twins were included in analyses. Twins were given $5 each for their participation. Ages of these twin pairs ranged from 6–53 and analyses were conducted to ensure that there were no significant differences between the age, ethnic, or sex composition of the MZ and DZ subgroups (see Table 1).

Materials

Twins aged 6–11 completed the three measures described here with the assistance of their parents. Twins aged 12 and older completed those questionnaires and several additional measures on their own. Packets were mailed to twins living outside the area and were administered in the lab for twins living locally. The questionnaires relevant to this report are the University of Illinois Twin Questionnaire, the Edinburgh Handedness Inventory, and the CFT.

Twin zygosity was determined using information from the University of Illinois Twin Questionnaire which was created by combining zygosity questionnaires developed by Goldsmith (1991), Magnus, Berg, and Nance (1983), Sarna, Kaprio, Sistonen, and Koskenvuo (1978), Nichols and Bilbro (1966), and Cederlof, Friberg, Jonsson, and Kaij (1961). Agreement between blood typing and questionnaire-based diagnosis of zygosity has varied from 93% (Nichols & Bilbro, 1966) to 98% (Magnus et al., 1983).

TABLE 1
Demographics

Group	MZ	DZ
No. of Twin Pairs	31	20
Age		
M	18.4	15.6
SD	10.9	9.6
Sex (% female)	66.7	60.0
Race (% caucasian)	83.9	95.0

All tests for zygosity effects were not significant at $\alpha = .05$.

Zygosity classification was based on guidelines adapted from Goldsmith (1991) and Sarna et al. (1978). Responses to questions such as the twins' likelihood of being confused as children and whether the twins were "as alike as two peas in a pod when younger" were compared. Sarna et al. (1978) found that agreement between twins for these two responses led to accurate classification of 93% of their twins. Four independent trained raters made zygosity ratings for each twin pair. All four raters agreed on zygosity classification for 95% of same-sex twin pairs. If all four raters did not agree that a particular twin pair was either MZ or DZ, the twin pair was eliminated from analyses.

Handedness was determined using a version of the Edinburgh Handedness Inventory (Oldfield, 1971) which consists of 10 items assessing hand preference for several activities. Participants were considered to be right-handed if they indicated both a preference to write with the right hand and an overall tendency to use their right hand more than their left.

Perceptual asymmetry was measured with the CFT (for further details, see Levy et al., 1983a,b). The CFT is a booklet consisting of 36 pages of two chimeric faces, one on top and one on the bottom. Each face is split such that for one face the left half is smiling while the right half is neutral, and for the other the right half is smiling while the left half is neutral. The composite faces on a single page are mirror images. Faces are counterbalanced for order and location (top, bottom) of left and right smiles, and for the side of the poser's face that was used to derive the expression. Participants were instructed to judge which face looked happier (top, bottom, or neither).

Item asymmetries on the task are not affected by top/bottom location of the smile-left chimera, by whether the smile was produced by the left or right side of the poser's face, by whether an item appears in the first or second half of the task, or by a poser's handedness (Levy et al., 1983b). As described earlier, the CFT has been found to be a reliable and valid measure of hemispatial biases (Kim & Levine, 1991, 1992; Kim et al., 1990; Levy et al., 1983b; Wirsen et al., 1990).

An asymmetry score on the CFT was calculated for each participant by subtracting left-face-smiling from right-face-smiling choices, and dividing by 36 (see Levy et al., 1983a for a complete rationale of this scoring procedure). The more negative the score, the greater the left hemispatial bias, and the more positive the score, the greater the right hemispatial bias. The more individuals are biased to the left side of space, the more the inferred right hemisphere relative to left hemisphere activity, and vice versa.

RESULTS

Preliminary Analyses

Analyses were conducted to ensure that assumptions would be met for twin study methodology (Eaves, Eysenck, & Martin, 1989). Mean age and variance did not differ between MZ and DZ twin pairs. Levene's test for equality of variances for CFT scores showed no difference in the variances of the MZ and

DZ scores, $F(115) = 2.62$, $P > .05$. There were no significant effects of birth order on mean or variance, $t(49) = -.42$, $P > .05$. An ANOVA to assess gender and zygosity effects on mean CFT scores indicated a main effect for gender, $F(1,100) = 12.29$, $P < .01$, in which males demonstrated much smaller asymmetry scores than did females (see Table 2). No effect was found for zygosity, $F(1,100) < 1$.

Heritability Analyses

Several different methods were used to examine whether CFT scores were genetically influenced. First, difference score analyses were conducted. We compared the means of the within-twin-pair absolute difference scores for MZ and DZ twins. Not only was there not a statistically significant difference between the means, but there was not even a trend for MZ twin pairs to be more similar than DZ twin pairs (see Table 3). Second, intraclass correlations (ICCs) were used to measure within-twin-pair resemblance. Both MZ and DZ ICCs were near zero, indicating no within-twin-pair resemblance (see Table 3). Furthermore, as the DZ ICC was larger than the MZ ICC, a heritability coefficient could not be generated. Finally, as females had somewhat more representative CFT scores than did males, the same analyses described previously were conducted for females alone. Again, there was a trend for MZ twin pairs to be less similar than DZ twin pairs and ICCs were near zero, precluding generation of a heritability coefficient.

The results of these analyses suggest that genes do not influence patterns of perceptual asymmetry. However, the aforementioned analyses have limited power to detect genetic effects that might be masked by interactions, such as gene × age or gene × gender. Therefore, a series of hierarchical multiple

TABLE 2
Mean CFT Scores by Sex and Zygosity

Zygosity	Males	Sex Females	Total
MZ			
M	−.04	−.47	−.33
SD	.56	.48	.54
DZ			
M	−.18	−.47	−.35
SD	.42	.50	.48
Total			
M	−.10	−.47	−.34
SD	.50	.48	.52

TABLE 3
Heritability Analyses

Group	MZ	DZ
Absolute Mean Difference Scores		
M	.61	.53
SD	.51	.43
ICCs	−.02	.12

Higher absolute mean difference scores indicate less within-twin-pair resemblance. More positive ICCs indicate more within-twin-pair resemblance.

regression (HMR) analyses following steps outlined by Rose (1988) were also conducted. Consistent with the results just described, there was no evidence for a gene main effect or for a genetic interaction with any other variable (e.g. age, gender).

Having found that perceptual asymmetry appeared not to be genetically influenced when measured dimensionally, we explored whether a categorically defined perceptual asymmetry would be genetically influenced. At each of 41 different cut-off points ranging from +1 to −1, we categorised twins as having either "high" or "low" CFT scores. A twin was "high" if his/her score was greater than or equal to the cut-off point, and "low" if his/her score was less than the cut-off point. For example, when the cut-off point was −.30, a twin was considered to be "high" if he/she had a score greater than or equal to −.30 (e.g. .10) and "low" if he/she had a score less than −.30 (e.g. −.55). We then established, at each different cut-off point, which of the twin pairs had concordant CFT scores, and which twin pairs had discordant CFT scores. A twin pair was considered concordant if both twins were categorised as "high" or if both twins were categorised as "low". A twin pair was considered discordant if one twin was categorised as "high" and one twin was categorised as "low".

As can be seen in Fig. 1, the MZ and DZ concordance rates are quite similar. As expected, when the CFT cut-off point is extremely high or low, almost all twin pairs are concordant, as almost everyone gets categorised as "high" at one end and "low" at the other end. For example, when the cut-off point is high (e.g. .90), almost all of the twin pairs are concordant because almost all of the twins have CFT scores below the cut-off point. When the cut-off point is low (e.g. −.90), almost all of the twin pairs are concordant because almost all of the twins have CFT scores above the cut-off point. As the cut-off points approach the middle of the range of CFT scores (e.g. −.5 to +.3) and the number of twins with CFT scores below the cut-off point is approximately

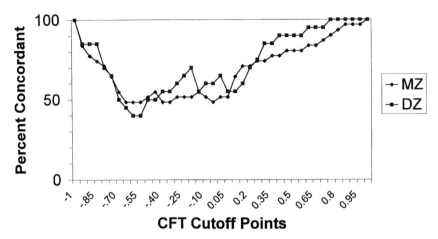

FIG. 1.   MZ and DZ concordance rates for CFT scores at different cut-off points.

equal to the number of twins with CFT scores above the cut-off point, concordance rates are approximately 50%. As can be seen in Fig. 1, there are about three times as many cut-off points for which the DZ concordance rate is greater than the MZ concordance rate. Also, there are no significant differences at cut-off points for which the MZ concordance rate is greater than DZ concordance rate.

Finally, exploratory analyses were conducted to assess whether the strength (independent of direction) of CFT scores was genetically influenced. All of the analyses described earlier (i.e. ICCs, difference scores, HMRs, concordance rates) were repeated for strength of CFT scores. These analyses were conducted using two different strengths of CFT asymmetry scores. First the analyses were conducted using the absolute value of the CFT score as the measure of strength of CFT asymmetry (e.g. a twin with a CFT score of –.400 or +.400 would have a strength of CFT asymmetry score of .400). The analyses were then repeated using the absolute value of the CFT score minus –.303 (–.303 being the CFT mean provided by Levy et al., 1983a) as the measure of strength of CFT asymmetry (e.g. a twin with a CFT score of –.303 would have a strength of CFT asymmetry score of zero, whereas a twin with a CFT score of –.103 or –.503 would have a strength of CFT asymmetry score of .200). These analyses yielded a pattern of results similar to those for direction of CFT asymmetry, again suggesting that CFT asymmetry is not genetically influenced.[2]

---

[2] When strength of CFT asymmetry was defined as the absolute value of the CFT score, ICCs for MZ and DZ twin pairs were .21 and .27, respectively, suggesting a small degree of non-genetic shared familiality. This familiality effect, however, was not found when the strength of the CFT asymmetry score was defined as the absolute value of the CFT score minus –.303.

Analyses to Ensure Representativeness of Data

All heritability analyses for direction and strength of CFT asymmetry indicated no genetic influence. To help rule out the possibility that this was a unique sample, we examined height, a variable that has been well established to have high heritability. If our analyses failed to yield a high heritability estimate for height, then it would appear that our sample is not representative of other samples. If, on the other hand, these analyses yielded a high heritability estimate for height, it would suggest that the low heritability estimate for the CFT scores is not simply due to an overall low level of heritability in our sample. Height scores for twins 18 and older, adjusted for age and gender, revealed an expected degree of heritability[3], $h^2 = 2 \ (.97-.60) = .74$ using the formula 2 $(r_{MZ}-r_{DZ})$, where r = the ICCs of MZ or DZ twin pairs respectively.

Analyses were also conducted to determine whether CFT scores in this sample were representative of other samples. The overall mean CFT score, −.34 (n = 102), was consistent with results obtained by Levy et al. (1983a) who found a mean score of −.303 (n = 111). Also, similar to other studies, 75% of the sample yielded CFT scores in the expected direction (bias for the left side of space; e.g. Levy et al., 1983a). Finally, a reliability check on the CFT indicated high internal consistency for all, younger, and older twins (Cronbach's alpha = .92, .83, and .95 respectively).

DISCUSSION

The results of this study indicate that, similar to direction of handedness, between-person variation in perceptual asymmetry as measured by the CFT does not appear to be genetically influenced. Also, like most other characteristics, it appears that CFT asymmetry is not accounted for by non-genetic *shared* familial factors but rather is influenced by *non-shared* factors that are unique to each twin.

In contrast to what we found for CFT asymmetry, between-person variation in many aspects of human functioning, such as cognitive abilities, personality characteristics, and psychiatric disorders, is genetically influenced. This is interesting because perceptual asymmetry is associated with the former set of variables. Our results, showing that CFT asymmetry is not influenced in the same way as is personality/psychopathology, suggest that there is not a set of genetic factors that influence both CFT asymmetry and personality/psycho-

---

[3] Height heritability scores for twins of all ages, however, were not within the expected range. Although the MZ ICC (.99) appeared within normal range, the DZ ICC (.95) remained high despite age and gender corrections. It may be the case that DZ ICCs are exceptionally high because age has a great effect on height between the ages of 6–18. This would make it possible for twin pairs within the same age group to look much more similar to each other than to others of a different age. Thus, the extremely strong effect of age on height could not be adjusted.

pathology. Our results also suggest that CFT asymmetry is not influenced by shared family or shared environmental factors. What then could account for the association between personality/psychopathology and individual differences in CFT asymmetry? The only remaining explanation for CFT asymmetry being associated with personality/psychopathology is that they are both influenced by common environmental factors. Examples of factors that might contribute to both personality/psychopathology and CFT asymmetry are exposure to viruses and birth stress. Both virus exposure and birth stress have been posited to play a role in personality/psychopathology and cognitive functioning (e.g. Hall & Smith, 1996; Kramer, Allen, & Gergen, 1995; Levander, Schalling, & Levander, 1989; Machon, Mednick, & Huttunen, 1997; Schmaling & Jones, 1996). Interestingly, birth stress has also been posited to play a role in handedness (e.g. Coren, 1994, 1995; Fox, 1985).

Although zygosity misclassification and the inclusion of a wide range of ages in our sample could conceivably have influenced our results, these factors cannot account for our findings. First, previous studies using similar classification methods have demonstrated high degrees of accuracy in zygosity classification (e.g. Magnus et al., 1983; Nichols & Bilbro, 1966). We also obtained expected familiality and heritability estimates for height. Furthermore, misclassification of zygosity would only affect the magnitude of the difference between MZ and DZ ICCs. It would not cause near zero estimates of familiality for both MZ and DZ twin pairs. Second, given the wide variation in ages in our sample, it is possible that traditional age corrections for computing heritability estimates were not strong enough to counteract the effects of this variation. Such effects, however, would ordinarily be expected to inflate the ICCs used to estimate heritability, not deflate them. Thus, age effects alone could not account for the near zero ICCs.

Our results suggest that genes do not play a strong or simple role in influencing between-person variation in CFT asymmetry. MZ and DZ ICCs would likely be greater than zero if genes were playing a large role. However, due to the size of our sample, we had somewhat limited power to detect small direct genetic effects or more complicated interactions. If CFT asymmetry is influenced by complicated genetic mechanisms as has been proposed for handedness (e.g. Annett, 1978, 1985, 1996; McManus, 1985), our method of analysis could underestimate the heritability of CFT asymmetry. Thus it is possible that genes may be playing a small and/or a more complicated role which may be worth investigating in future studies. It would be interesting to examine interactions not only with age and gender, but also with environmental factors, as these types of interactions have been noted by others (Reiss et al., 1995).

In conclusion, it appears that between-person variation in CFT asymmetry, like direction of handedness, is influenced by either non-genetic or complicated genetic mechanisms. Future research might seek to identify which genetic and non-genetic mechanisms influence the between-person variation of handedness and perceptual asymmetry. For example, do the mechanisms that contribute to direction and strength of handedness also contribute to direction and strength of perceptual asymmetry?

Manuscript received 8 July 1997
Revised manuscript received 27 February 1998

REFERENCES

Annett, M. (1978). *A single gene explanation of right and left handedness and brainedness.* Coventry, UK: Lanchester Polytechnic.

Annett, M. (1985). *Left, right, hand and brain: The Right Shift theory.* Hove, UK: Lawrence Erlbaum Associates Ltd.

Annett, M. (1996). In defence of the Right Shift theory. *Perceptual and Motor Skills, 82,* 115–137.

Banich, M.T., Elledge, V.C., & Stolar, N. (1992). Variations in lateralized processing among right-handers: Effects on patterns of cognitive performance. *Cortex, 28,* 273–288.

Berenbaum, H., & Prince, J.D. (1994). Alexithymia and the interpretation of emotion-relevant information. *Cognition and Emotion, 8,* 231–244.

Berenbaum, H., & Williams, M. (1994). Extraversion, hemispatial bias, and eyeblink rates. *Personality and Individual Differences, 17,* 849–852.

Bradshaw, J.L., & Nettleton, N.C. (1983). *Human cerebral asymmetry.* Englewood Cliffs, NJ: Prentice-Hall.

Bruder, G.E. (1995). Cerebral laterality and psychopathology: Perceptual and event-related potential asymmetries in affective and schizophrenic disorders. In R.J. Davidson & K. Hugdahl (Eds.), *Brain asymmetry* (pp.661–691). Cambridge, MA: MIT Press.

Carey, G., & DiLalla, D.L. (1994). Personality and psychopathology: Genetic perspectives. *Journal of Abnormal Psychology, 103,* 32–43.

Carlier, M., Spitz, E., Vacher-Lavenu, M., Villeger, P., Martin, B., & Michel, F. (1996). Manual performance and laterality in twins of known chorion type. *Behavior Genetics, 26,* 409–417.

Cederlof, R., Friberg, L., Jonsson, E., & Kaij, L. (1961). Studies on similarity diagnosis in twins with the aid of mailed questionnaires. *Acta Genetica, 11,* 338–362.

Charman, D.K. (1979). Do different personalities have different hemispheric asymmetries? A brief communique of an initial experiment. *Cortex,15,* 655–657.

Corballis, M.C., & Beale, I.L. (1976). *The psychology of left and right.* Hillsdale, NJ: Lawrence Erlbaum Associates Inc.

Coren, S. (1992). *The left hander syndrome: The causes and consequences of left handedness.* New York: The Free Press.

Coren, S. (1994). Twinning is associated with an increased risk of left-handedness and inverted writing hand postures. *Early Human Development, 40,* 23–27.

Coren, S. (1995). Family patterns in handedness: Evidence for indirect inheritance mediated by birth stress. *Behavior Genetics, 25,* 517–524.

Derom, C., Thiery, E., Vlietinck, R., Loos, R., & Derom, R. (1996). Handedness in twins according to zygosity and chorion type: A preliminary report. *Behavior Genetics, 26,* 407–408.

Eaves, L.J., Eysenck, H.J., & Martin, N.G. (1989). The classical approach: Early twin studies of personality. In *Genes, Culture and Personality: An Empirical Approach* (pp. 19–41). San Diego, CA: Academic Press Inc.

Fox, N. (1985). The relationship to perinatal birth status to handedness: A prospective study. Special issue: "The organization of cerebral lateral functioning during infancy". *Infant Mental Health Journal, 6,* 175–184.

Goldsmith, H.H. (1991). A zygosity questionnaire for young twins: A research note. *Behavior Genetics, 21*, 257–269.

Green, J., Morris, R.D., Epstein, C.M., West, P.D., & Engler, H.F.J. (1992). Assessment of the relationship of cerebral hemisphere arousal asymmetry to perceptual asymmetry. *Brain and Cognition, 20*, 264–279.

Hall, S.R., & Smith, A.P. (1996). Behavioral effects of infectious mononucleosis. *Neuropsychobiology, 33*, 202–209.

Heller, W. (1991). Hemispatial biases in children on the Draw-A-Person Test. *Developmental Neuropsychology, 7*, 151–160.

Heller, W., Etienne, M.A., & Miller, G.A. (1995). Patterns of perceptual asymmetry in depression and anxiety: Implications for neuropsychological models of emotion and psychopathology. *Journal of Abnormal Psychology, 104*, 327–333.

Hellige, J.B., Bloch, M.I., Cowin, E.L., Eng, T.L., Eviatar, Z., & Sergent, V. (1994). Individual variation in hemispheric asymmetry: Multitask study of effects related to handedness and sex. *Journal of Experimental Psychology, 123*(3), 235–256.

Hoptman, M., & Levy, J. (1988). Perceptual asymmetries in left-and right-handers for cartoon and real faces. *Brain and Cognition, 8*, 178–188.

Kim, H. (1994). Distributions of hemispheric asymmetry in left-handers and right-handers: Data from perceptual asymmetry studies. *Neuropsychology, 8*, 148–159.

Kim, H., & Levine, S.C. (1991). Inferring patterns of hemispheric specialization for individual subjects from laterality data: A two-task criterion. *Neuropsychologia, 29*, 93–105.

Kim, H., & Levine, S.C. (1992). Variations in characteristic perceptual asymmetry: Modality specific and modality general components. *Brain and Cognition, 19*, 21–47.

Kim, H., Levine, S.C., & Kertesz, S. (1990). Are variations among subjects in lateral asymmetry real individual differences or random error in measurement?: Putting variability in its place. *Brain and Cognition, 14*, 220–242.

Kramer, R.A., Allen, L., & Gergen, P. (1995). Health and social characteristics and children's cognitive functioning: Results from a national cohort. *American Journal of Public Health, 85*, 312–318.

Laland, K.N., Kumm, J., Van Horn, J.D., & Feldman, M.W. (1995). A gene-culture model of human handedness. *Behavior Genetics, 25*, 433–445.

Levander, M., Schalling, D., & Levander, S.E. (1989). Birth stress, handedness, and cognitive performance. *Cortex, 25*, 673–681.

Levy, J., Heller, W., Banich, M.T., & Burton, L.A. (1983a). Are variations among right-handed individuals in perceptual asymmetries causes by characteristic arousal differences between hemisphere? *Journal of Experimental Psychology: Human Perception and Performance, 9*, 329–359.

Levy, J., Heller, W., Banich, M.T., & Burton, L.A. (1983b). Asymmetries of perception in free viewing of chimeric faces. *Brain and Cognition, 2*, 404–419.

Levy, J., & Kueck, L. (1985). A right-hemisphere field advantage on a verbal free-vision test. *Brain and Cognition, 27*, 24–37.

Luh, K.E., Rueckert, L.M., & Levy, J. (1991). Perceptual asymmetries for free viewing of several types of chimeric stimuli. *Brain and Cognition, 16*, 83–103.

Machon, R.A., Mednick, S., & Huttunen, M.O. (1997). Adult major affective disorder after prenatal exposure to an influenza epidemic. *Archives of General Psychiatry, 54*, 322–328.

Magnus, P., Berg, K., & Nance, W.E. (1983). Predicting zygosity in Norwegian twin pairs born 1915–1960. *Clinical Genetics, 24*, 103–112.

McCartney, K., Harris, M.J., & Bernierni, F. (1990). Growing up and growing apart: A developmental meta-analysis of twin studies. *Psychological Bulletin, 107*, 226–237.

McManus, I.C. (1985). Handedness, language dominance and aphasia. *Psychological Medicine Monograph Supplement 8.* Cambridge: Cambridge University Press.

Nichols, R.C., & Bilbro, W.C. (1966). The diagnosis of twin zygosity. *Acta Genetica, 16*, 265–275.

Oldfield, R.C. (1971). The assessment and analysis of handedness: The Edinburgh Inventory. *Neuropsychologia, 9*, 97–113.

Orlebeke, J.F., Knol, D.L., Koopmans, J.R., Boomsma, D.I., & Bleker, O.P. (1996). Left-handedness in twins: Genes or environment? *Cortex, 32*, 479–490.

Reiss, D., Heatherington, M., Plomin, R., Howe, G.W., Simmens, S.J., Henderson, S.H., O'Connor, T.J., Bussell, D.A., Anderson, E.R., & Law, T. (1995). Genetic questions for environmental studies: Differential parenting and psychopathology in adolescence. *Archives of General Psychiatry, 52*, 925–936.

Rose, R.J. (1988). Genetic and environmental variance in content dimensions of the MMPI. *Journal of Personality and Social Psychology, 55*, 302–311.

Sarna, S., Kaprio, J., Sistonen, P., & Koskenvuo, M. (1978). Diagnosis of twin zygosity by mailed questionnaire. *Human Heredity, 28*, 241–254.

Schmaling, K.B., & Jones, J.F. (1996). MMPI profiles of patients with chronic fatigue syndrome. *Journal of Psychosomatic Research, 40*, 67–74.

Tressoldi, P.E. (1987). Visual hemispace differences reflect hemisphere asymmetries. *Neuropsychologia, 25*, 625–636.

Wirsen, A., Klinteberg, B.A., Levander, S., & Schalling, D. (1990). Differences in asymmetric perception of facial expression in free-vision chimeric stimuli and reaction time. *Brain and Cognition, 12*, 229–239.

Author Index

Ajuriaguerra, J. 265
Albajar, M. 245, 248
Allen, L. 308
Anderson, E.R. 308
Annett, M. 265, 266, 268, 271, 276, 281, 287, 288, 294, 295, 301, 308
Arey, L. 203
Asthana, H.S. 294
Atkinson, G. 282

Baden, J.M. 198
Bailly, S. 243
Bakan, P. 266, 280
Bancaud, J. 266, 280
Banich, M.T. 300, 301, 303, 307
Bankovi, G. 268, 270, 272–274, 277, 290
Barker, W.B. 268, 270, 272–274, 277–279
Bateson, W. 242
Bautzmann, H. 249
Beale, I.L. 301
Beere, D. 205
Belmonte, J.C.I. 201, 243, 245, 246
Berenbaum, H. 299, 301
Berg, K. 266, 268, 270–274, 276–279, 281, 282, 302, 308
Bergquist, H. 222
Bernierni, F. 301
Bertani, G. 249
Biddle, F.G. 263
Bilbro, W.C. 302, 308
Bleker, O.P. 268, 270, 272–274, 277, 279, 282, 290, 301
Bloch, M.I. 300
Blumberg, B. 201, 243, 245, 246
Bohn, H. 242
Boklage, C.E. 268, 270, 272–274, 277–279
Boomsma, D.K. 268, 270, 272–274, 277, 279, 282, 290, 301
Bourassa, D.C. 294
Bouterwek, H. 269
Bracha, H.S. 266
Bradshaw, J.L. 287, 294, 300
Brauns, A. 243
Brenci, G. 205
Bride, M. 243
Brown, N.A. 198, 242–244, 249, 294
Bruder, G.E. 301

Brueckner, M. 198, 201, 281
Bryant, P.J. 249
Bryant, S.V. 249
Bryden, M.P. 195, 258, 266, 267, 287, 288, 294, 295
Burn, J. 198, 201
Burton, L.A. 300, 301, 303, 307
Bussell, D.A. 308
Buss, K.A. 266, 268, 271, 276, 280

Caffarra, P. 195
Caffrey, E.A. 266, 268, 271, 276
Cardon, L.R. 258
Carey, G. 301
Carlier, M. 268, 270, 272–274, 277–279, 282, 290, 301
Carter-Saltzman, L. 266, 268, 270, 272–274, 277–279
Carton, A. 205
Castresana, A. 266, 280
Caubergh, M.A.A. 294
Cederlof, R. 282, 302
Chamberlain, H.D. 266
Chang, P.C. 269
Chapman, D.B. 198
Charman, D.K. 301
Cheng, A.M.S. 243, 245, 246, 248
Choe, S. 201, 243, 245, 246
Cidis, M. 205
Clark, C.M. 269
Cleaton-Jones, P. 205
Coffaro, C.M. 263
Collignon, J. 201
Collins, R.L. 257, 262, 263, 265, 294
Cooke, J. 199, 201, 203, 243, 246
Copeland, N.G. 198
Copenhaver, W.M. 243
Corballis, M.C. 195, 210, 243, 251, 266, 287, 294, 301
Coren, S. 266, 268, 271, 276, 280, 287, 288, 294, 295, 301, 308
Cornish, K.M. 195
Cowin, E.L. 300
Cubelli, R. 195

Dahlberg, G. 268, 270, 272–274, 277–279, 290
Danos, M.C. 246, 248

313

315

317

Subject Index